WHAT ARE PEOPLE SAYING ABOUT

"GOD, IF YOU ARE
UP THERE, DO YOU CARE?"

What a privilege it has been for me to know this dear saint in the Lord for the past 20 years as the current pastor of her "home sending church family". Rosalie Ranquist has been for us a living, breathing example of what our great God might be pleased to do through one who willingly and whole-hearted gives her life to the service of our Master. Rosalie has often encouraged us over the years to know that the Lord is not nearly as concerned with our upbringing, education or even natural abilities as He is with our consecrated avail-ability. And now, thankfully, after the prodding of many who have known her over the years, she has finally committed to writing the story of her life from various addictions and hope-less despair to that of joyous, faith-filled, adventuresome, international fruitfulness for the Kingdom in dozens of tribal groups throughout Asia, Africa and South America. It is a story that will prove to be inspiring and challenging for you to live your life in keeping with 1 Corinthians 15:58—one of Rosalie's life's verses.

David M. Moynihan, M.Div.,
Pastor of the First Baptist Church
of Waterford, CT

When the LORD said to Abraham, "Is anything too hard for the LORD?" (Genesis 18:14), His question proclaimed a fundamental truth that has touched every subsequent gen-eration. Could the LORD then transform an obstreperous elementary school dropout into an indispensable literacy consultant, encompassing 70 tribal languages scattered throughout the globe? Such is the story of Rosalie Ranquist, an amazing woman, whom I first met in the of her Christ-appointed land, Pap is as exciting as it is readable! It will inspire your heart and life to "trust in the LORD," even among the most harrowing circumstances.

Gene L. Jeffries, Th.D.
Assistant Professor of Theology
Liberty Baptist Theological Seminary
Lynchburg, Virginia

"This autobiography is a testimony to the grace of God at work through the life of Rosalie Ranquist. My wife Donna and I have known Rosalie for 50 years. We met her at the beginning of the 1960s as a young believer with a heart to serve and honor our Lord. We have had the privilege of maintaining contact with her during this half a century of her growing in grace and being used in strategic ministry. I commend this book to you for your encouragement as a believer. We are all called to fulfill our part in our Lord's commission to make disciples of all nations. Rosalie has modeled a life of commitment to her Lord and Savior.

I count it a high privilege to know this servant of our Lord Jesus Christ. If you are a believer, may you be encouraged in your walk with our Lord. If not, may you come to know the Savior that Rosalie came to know, the one who not only saved her but changed her for His glory and honor."

Gary F. Coombs, D.Miss, PhD
President, Southern California Seminary, El Cajon, CA

Few people know Rosalie Ranquist as well as I do. It was an incredible privilege to be her co-worker with NTM and to share a home with her for many years. To tell all the ways that she has blessed and impacted my life would necessitate writing a book of my own! Space limits me to this:

Rosalie never uses her background as an excuse for her former behavior, but believes the simple truth that *God transforms lives.* She does, of course, recognize the challenges that are a result of years of rejection and ridicule. For example, early in our relationship, Rosalie found it difficult to accept words of appreciation or a compliment as sincere. "You're making fun of me!" was often her first response. That was problematic! But we recognized the source of that attitude; she faced it, and—by God's grace—she changed. So, my dear friend, Rosalie, I know you can accept this as genuine and heart-felt: *Thank you for writing this wonderful book!* Once again, my life has been blessed by your obedience to the Lord, in your willingness to re-live the pain of the past—as well as the victory of the present—for His glory. And I am confident that each of you who reads this account will echo these words: Thank you, Rosalie.

Carol (Gutwein) Kaptain,
Linguist and Bible Translator

GOD, IF YOU ARE UP THERE, DO YOU CARE?

An Autobiography

By

Rosalie Ranquist

God If You Are Up There Do You Care?

by Rosalie Ranquist

Printed in the United States of America

ISBN 9781622300532

Unless otherwise indicated, Bible quotations are taken from the King James Version.

www.xulonpress.com

Dedication

This book is lovingly dedicated to

Mrs. Pauline Stanley

a dear Christian friend in Maine, who from the first time she heard my story, many years ago, has encouraged me to put my life's story in writing. Thank you for relentlessly challenging me.

Table of Contents

Forward

*L*ife seems too unfair at times, especially for a child who is left at a foster home because her father can no longer take care of his children. Rosalie is forced to grow up quickly and must deal with loneliness, rejection and poor choices. Her high energy and determination work both for and against her as she seeks to find meaning and purpose in life. In this riveting personal story, Rosalie shares how God graciously reached out to her and gave her a new identity.

I have been blessed to know Rosalie for nearly twenty years and have witnessed her tenacious commitment to serve Christ as an international literacy consultant. I highly recommend this autobiography to you, knowing that when you put it down you'll be supercharged by what God can do with a life that is willing to serve Him. If you, like Rosalie, are wondering if God can use you with the emotional scars that life has dealt you, reading this book will give you hope.

Rosalie is one of the heroes of the faith "of whom the world [is] not worthy" (Hebrews 11:38a). Now in her seventies, Rosalie's energy and passion are still contagious. When she comes to my office it's hard to contain her for more than a few minutes before she's off on a "mission" once again.

Larry M. Brown
Chairman and CEO
NTM USA

Introduction

*F*or more than twenty years, friends have nagged me to write my life's story. Obviously, I didn't take them too seriously until recently. Finally, I decided to allow the wonder of voice recognition technology to translate my spoken words onto the digital page. That was quite entertaining since the program heard everything I said but had a hard time dealing with my Maine accent!

The initial manuscript was like an overgrown garden that needed much attention. My friends Jeannine Orr, who helped in the early stages, and Nancy Harris and Glenda Coy who stayed with me to the end, patiently plowing through the rough draft, ridding it of large weeds and unnecessary repetition. They told me I needed an editor. Rhoda Johnson kindly consented. She helped me to prune the bushes, clear the pathways, and fertilize the plants. Soon my story began to bloom.

Feeling more confident, I gladly asked others to read the manuscript. Thank you to Pastor Dave Moynihan, Larry Brown, Gary Coombs and Carol (Gutwein) Kaptain for their insightful comments. I appreciate Ruth Brendle and Naomi Libby for helping with the final proofreading.

Andy Daniels competently did the layout, while John Pierce provided the cover photo that so aptly captures my intent.

Now there's no more need to nag. You're holding my story! May it change you in some way, and help you to celebrate your own life's story.

Rosalie Ranquist
Sanford, Florida
March 2012

PS. I've omitted the names of some people and places in the early part of my story. This is done out of love and respect for them. A couple of my tribal friends' names have also been changed.

Chapter 1

Life's Rough Beginning

*L*ife for me began on a small island off the coast of Maine, where our house overlooked the ocean and people earned a livelihood mostly from lobster fishing. I was the seventh child born to my father and mother, Charles and Clementine Ranquist.

My mother at age 29 became very sick. She was eight months pregnant with her eighth child, but heavy snow and ice made it impossible for the doctor to reach her. The harbor on Swan's Island had frozen over, requiring the Coast Guard cutter to come to break up the ice so that Mom could be taken to a hospital on the mainland.

For three hours they battled heavy seas and high winds. By the time they arrived at the hospital, Mom's skin was turning black. She had a ruptured appendix and severe peritonitis was setting in. The doctors told my dad that she would live only two days at the most. With Dad's consent, they performed surgery to save the baby. But the little girl didn't survive. My mother lived two more days so I never knew her. I was 15 months old when she passed away.

Dad was a steamboat engineer, so having seven children ranging in age from 1 to 12 posed tremendous challenges for him. The steamboat he worked on carried mail and supplies to other small islands off the coast of Maine, and would sometimes remain overnight in the main port. So what would happen to us on the nights he was away?

When my mother realized she was dying, she asked my father to keep us kids together. She also asked Dad to keep my brother, who was the oldest, on the steamboat with him. Dad tried to fulfill her request, but it was impossible. So for a short time family members and friends on the island helped out, with each child going to a different home. I later learned that an older couple with no children wanted to adopt me, but my dad, abiding by my mother's dying wishes, refused their offer, even though he knew he could not care for me.

After several months, Dad contacted "The Home of the Little Wanderers", which was a charitable organization that helped families place children in foster homes. As a result, my three brothers went to live with a foster family in a small rural town on the mainland. My two older sisters and I found ourselves in a foster home in a small mainland city.

Vivid memories are easy for me to recall from age 5 onward. Hard work is one of them. From the outset I was given chores that were beyond my age and strength. An obvious scar on my left hand reminds me daily that I nearly cut through the main artery and thumb cartilage.

I was probably about 8 years old and had come home for lunch, as we did sometimes during the school week, but this day I must have done something wrong, which wasn't unusual. The punishment was to chop kindling wood. But instead of an ax, I was given a new, sharp hatchet to attack a large, round piece of wood. A few chops later, the hatchet hit a knot in the wood, bounced off and landed across the base of my thumb. Instead of sending me back to school, my foster dad rushed me to the doctor's office.

The older doctor worked hurriedly to stop the bleeding and stitch up the severe gash. My nerves jittered and my face grimaced as he pulled the skin tight to tie the knot in each stitch. He didn't freeze the wound. But it was my foster dad who had a worse time than me. He was holding on to me, as the doctor requested, when suddenly I saw him start to drop to the floor, but he was able to quickly grab on to a chair and sit down. I couldn't understand why he would faint when I was the one going through the ordeal and feeling the pain! That gave me something to brag about, but not around home.

Immediate obedience was expected on every chore assigned to me. Often I had to carry large stainless steel or galvanized buckets of water for some of the animals. I could barely lift them off the floor, but I had no choice. Disobedience meant another whipping—with a belt, a yardstick, or sometimes a cane, whichever was handy at the moment. Black and blue bruises and broken skin were common marks on my body; the steel-tipped cane left a scar under my left eye for a long time.

My foster mother usually kept a yard stick at the table, mostly for my benefit. I did not disappoint her. When the family sat around the table for a meal, my sisters often begged me, "Please be good." They would usually hang their heads because they were afraid that I'd snicker if I looked at them. Of course their actions prompted me to want to look at them or, even worse, to burst out laughing, which happened more often than not. I must have been a brat and deserving of many of the consequences.

By now you may realize that I was a hyper and mischievous child. In today's world my behavior would probably be labeled as an ADHD disorder. That may have been true of me…and it may still be! My school days were filled with challenges too, which I'll tell you about next.

Chapter 2

A Challenging Childhood

*B*ecause my birthday was near the end of September, I began school a year late in what was then called sub-primary. I remember that we basically played learning games, which were easy for me. So there was plenty of opportunity for mischief.

Early on I began to mimic animal sounds, people's voices, or other strong sounds. My life-like imitations amazed others, and even myself, especially when I added a new sound to my repertoire.

One time in third grade my teacher became irritated with me when she heard me making noises. "Rosalie," she said, "come here and stand in front of the class." So I obeyed, not sure what would happen, but thinking she might want to spank me. "Rosalie," she said, "now I want you to make every noise the students ask you to make." Yippee, I thought. Now I can do what I wanted to do.

One by one the teacher allowed the kids to ask me to mimic a sound. So I filled the classroom with imitations of pigs, trains, birds, cars, horses, roosters, babies, and more. What a fun time it turned out to be! Instead of punishment, the teacher unintentionally rewarded me. My classmates were thrilled with the entertainment. But never again did the teacher ask me to make sounds, which was a great disappointment to the kids and me.

A year or so later I became intimately acquainted with the coat closet in the long hallway that ran parallel to the back of the classroom. There was a door between the closet and where the kids headed when the bell sounded to end class. Some teachers thought it beneficial to banish me to the closet as a form of punishment. Obviously, I managed to frustrate them too often in class.

Even a clothes closet could not confine me. On occasion I managed to sneak out of it and run down the fire drill stairway into the school yard, where I would play for a while and return to my hideaway before class ended. I even remember sneaking home one day. My foster mom must not have been there or I would have gotten a beating. Somehow I got back to the closet in time. As far as I know, the teacher never knew of my escapades.

Since school did not challenge me academically, I had too much time on my hands, which posed a huge problem for this overactive kid. It amazed me that my report card almost always showed A and A+ grades, with one glaring exception: conduct scored F. This continued through the fifth grade.

I dreaded taking my report card home. Typically, my foster mother would stand me in the middle of the kitchen floor and, with anyone else who was in the house as witnesses, she'd yell at me, "You are stupid." Or she'd shout, "There's something wrong with you!" She never acknowledged the high grades I'd received. Added to that would be a good licking with a stick of some sort.

As a result I began to believe that I was foolish and stupid. Her words were continually hurtful and distasteful. They pierced my soul and continued to affect me into my teenage years. By the time I left home, I was convinced that I was dumb. This developed into a serious inferiority complex that became part of me until later in life when everything changed. Even now, its ugly head imposes itself on me from time to time, but I have learned how to deal with it.

Chapter 3

Too Tough For Me

Summertime of my ninth year found me escaping from people on different occasions. I'd head off to a field a good distance away and lie down in the tall, lush grass. As I gazed at the blue sky and puffy white clouds, my eyes often filled with tears and my heart cried out, "God, if you are up there, do you care? Life is too tough for me. Why am I here? I don't want to be here." Of course, I kept my longings to myself. I'd get up, brush myself off, and head back to my foster home, determined not to let my heartache show.

Even though my childhood was unhappy, I am grateful that I had a roof over my head and plenty of food to eat. That's something many people during World War II did not have. Besides developing a strong work ethic, I also learned some useful skills.

My foster parents had a small farm with milk and beef cows, as well as sheep and pigs, plenty of ducks, geese, chickens, and rabbits. About the only things we needed to buy at the store were sugar, salt, flour, oil, and spices. Each summer there was a large garden to care for. My sisters and I worked hard pulling weeds, and later helped with picking or digging the vegetables. Next we helped with the cleaning and cutting process for canning. By fall the cellar was full of about everything that we would want or need until the next season.

Churning butter was another skill I began learning at a

young age. The churn tool was a long pole with a thick and heavy, round piece of wood attached to the bottom. My little arms ached as I kept lifting the rod up and down, but I was determined not to complain. Later, we got a modern churn—a good-sized, round barrel-bellied wooden container with a crank that had to be turned round and round at a good pace. However, it also often proved too heavy a chore for my young body.

Another modern piece of equipment that pleased me was the milk separator. I didn't like milk but the heavy cream tasted so good on my cereal and in hot drinks. My dislike for milk may have been a result of punishment I received for squirting milk straight from the cow I was milking at someone else, instead of making sure it went directly into the bucket. That was a no-no! Right after that I was given hot milk to drink that came straight from the cow. I didn't like that a little bit!

The hard labor started to show in muscle growth in my right arm. This embarrassed me at times. But on other occasions I liked to display my strength, especially when it came to bullies at school. Often I went to the rescue of some helpless kid. Sometimes I got the worst end of the encounter, escaping with bruises. Nevertheless, I found it satisfying to protect the picked-on school kids. Even to this day I tend to be drawn to the underdog.

Often I was not allowed to play with other kids because I had barn work to do. But I remember one snowy evening when I was finally free to go tobogganing with the older kids on a little hill in the back field. We slid down with glee on a homemade heavy zinc toboggan. Then I, the little kid, was given the big toboggan to carry back up the hill.

My "butter churning" muscles helped me take on the challenge and show the kids how strong I was. But I became too confident. Next trip up the hill the heavy toboggan folded back and landed on my nose, which began to bleed profusely as I dashed home. The bleeding stopped but the pain didn't. My face became swollen and changed to a stunning black and blue around my eyes, nose, and cheeks. But I was not taken to a doctor. A slightly dented scar marked the memory on the outside. Inside, I became self-conscious about it as I got older. The scar and the results of it weren't taken care of until 1976.

On another occasion the bigger kids left a mark on me of a different kind. We were pretending to be a train, with each person holding on to the clothes of the person in front of them. For some reason I was put at the end—the caboose, I suppose. The train picked up speed, and it was fun until someone stumbled and we all landed in a pile—with me on the bottom!

Suddenly I felt great pain. Evidently, one of the older kids had stood on my collar bone when she got up. I screamed and screamed with pain. This brought my foster mother running to the scene. She told me to stand up. "Lift your arms," she yelled. I could not do so, no matter how hard I tried. "Lift your arms," she shouted again. "I can't," I cried. But she did not listen. "You cry baby," she scolded, "stop it!"

Soon afterward, I was rushed to the hospital for x-rays. The result: multiple fractures in my collar bone. A heavy plaster cast was put on me from the shoulder to below the rib cage. My skin itched inside that restraint for several weeks. The summer was hot and I was uncomfortable.

Appendicitis pain became familiar to me some time later. I experienced two appendicitis attacks, and both times some of my classmates had to carry me home from school. The doctor told me to be careful about lifting heavy things, but one day I was sent to clear the corner of the cellar, which meant picking up some large stones. Shortly after this I was rushed to the hospital with what they called "red hot appendix." The doctor operated immediately. I ended up staying in the hospital for ten days. There was an outbreak of scarlet fever at the same time so no one was allowed to visit me. Maybe that was good as it kept me from getting into trouble, thus no need for spankings!

For a brief time after arriving home, unusual kindness was shown to me. I was asked what special food I'd like to have for my first dinner. That was easy. "String beans," I replied. I loved to eat the raw string beans when I was doing the spring weeding; I'd hide in the furrows and munch on them for a treat. Now I would be served my favorite food on a plate.

However, the familiar pattern soon resumed and I got into more trouble, this time at Sunday school at the Baptist church. I found the class boring, so I'd imitate the teacher's voice, or try to get other kids into trouble. The teacher gave me extra assignments to do as a challenge, but to no avail. My photographic memory seemed to be a hindrance rather than a help as a child. So I was glad when my foster parents offered me a hard physical job to do on Sunday instead. I preferred to clean out the stinking manure from the hen pens, or whitewash the hen pen walls, rather than sit in class.

My foster parents must have despaired of me ever behaving. One time I unwittingly asked for punishment at the dinner table. I was bragging about how many ears of corn I could eat—twelve of them, I believe. Now this was end-of-season corn, so it was on the tough side, not sweet and tender. I'd forgotten about that detail. Anyhow, I ate and ate until I had to go to the bathroom and vomit. But there was still more corn on my plate. Everyone else was excused from the table, but my foster mom stayed there with the yardstick by her side, waiting for me to return. Sure enough, she made me eat every ear. My stomach ached. But my pride was not diminished. Her goal was to teach me to be quiet at the table; it didn't work.

My next boasting fest involved steak. We raised our own beef, and whenever it was on the menu, I was excited. I loved it fried in homemade butter. I can't remember exactly how much steak I claimed that I could eat, but I do remember the outcome. Soon I was running to the bathroom to regurgitate. Once more I was commanded to finish eating all that I'd heaped on my plate. It was a struggle, but I managed. Lesson learned! I don't recall ever going through that experience again.

Of many painful childhood memories, there are a few tender moments tucked away. My foster mom liked to have me cut her thick toenails after she soaked her feet. At some point during this procedure, she would ask me to sing the same song to her. Every time tears would start to trickle down her cheeks as she stared at me. "Rocking Alone In an Old Rocking Chair" is the song, written by Bob Mills. It goes like this:

Sitting alone in an old rocking chair,
I saw an old mother with silvery hair,
She looked so neglected by those who should care,
Rocking alone in an old rocking chair.

Her hands were all calloused and wrinkled and old,
A life of hard work was the story they told,
And I thought of angels when I saw her there,
Rocking alone in an old rocking chair.

Bless her old heart, do you think she complained,
Though life had been bitter she'd live it again,
And carry the cross that was more than her share,
Rocking alone in an old rocking chair.

It wouldn't take much to gladden her heart,
Just some small remembrance on somebody's part,
A letter would brighten her empty life there,
Rocking alone in an old rocking chair.

I know some children in an orphan home,
Who'd think they owned heaven if she were their own,
They'd never be willing to let her sit there,
Rocking alone in an old rocking chair.

I look at her and I think what a shame,
The ones that forgot her she still loves the same,
And I think of angels when I see her there,
Rocking alone in an old rocking chair.

My stepmother's tears touched me deep inside. It was a good feeling to think that I pleased her. I sometimes wondered if she'd been hurt as a child.

Chapter 4

From the Frying Pan Into the Fire

When I was 12 years old, the neighbors near our foster home complained to "The Home of the Little Wanderers" about the abuse that I and my older sister were experiencing. Our middle sister was treated well because she suffered with epilepsy caused from a baseball that had hit her square in the eye when she was younger. That organization then informed my father of our need to live somewhere else. Dad had rarely visited us—perhaps he couldn't afford to—so it surprised me when he chose to take us to live with him once again on Swan's Island, Maine.

Life was empty for my father without mom, so a few years later after she died, he married a young lady 18 years younger than he was and they had three children together. We found out we had a half-brother and two half-sisters. My half brother was the oldest and would start school that year. My two half-sisters were around 3 and 4 years of age. This was a new family with whom we'd need to become acquainted. In fact, I really didn't know my father either. My step-mother faced no small task, needing to adjust to my teenage sisters and my hyperactivity; I would soon turn 13 as well! This move to me was symbolically like the title of this chapter—"From the Frying Pan into the Fire."

When my father arrived to get us, we three girls could not fit into the car together. Guess who was left behind? Yes, me! My sisters were probably excited, but I felt so frightened and forsaken to be left alone without their support. I've often wondered if my dad intentionally left me behind so the family could have time to adjust without me. He knew I'd pose a challenge to them. As it turned out, I was treated quite well in the foster home during that time. I was glad. My excitement kept growing with the hope of my father coming to get me in a month's time.

When he arrived, we headed for the boat that would take us to the island, but I found I couldn't cope with new people around me. They seemed to be staring at me with a pathetic look. So I ran and hid behind a tree as tears came to my eyes. Dad persuaded me to come with him, but I was sure people were thinking I was dumb and foolish, or even funny looking. I hated feeling so self-conscious. Tears still come to my eyes, at times, when I think of all the devastating things I'd been told as a young child. I believed them.

My first night at home with my dad is etched forever on my memory. He was drunk and fighting with my stepmother. I don't know what brought that fight on, but I do know that I was frightened because he had a .22 rifle in his hand and they were struggling over it. I had never seen a drunken person before, which was another benefit for me having grown up in the foster home during my preteen years.

The new freedom that I gained brought new problems. I started smoking right away, and it soon became a serious habit. It displeased my father and he let me know it, but he never whipped me, probably because of the way I'd been treated all my life prior to that.

I worked for different people cleaning houses and doing chores; I even worked down at the boat wharf to make some spending money. The little money that I was paid was used to buy cigarettes and soda pop and sweet food. By then I was addicted to cigarettes, so sometimes when I didn't have money, I'd go to the neighbors' houses and pick up the long cigarette butts from their ash trays and smoke them.

My reputation as a hyper kid had preceded my arrival on the island. Even my grade 6 teacher who I'd soon come face-to-face with had been warned. She was kind to me even though it was a challenge for her to have me in the class. Once again I had too much time on my hands, so more often than not I was given what she thought was a difficult assignment to keep my mind occupied. It did work, but not all the time!

When she asked me to draw the faces of the different Presidents of the United States, that task held my attention for quite a while. I did have some art skills, but drawing faces was a challenge. Having to draw a map of Brazil and put in all the main rivers and tributaries was a greater challenge. But once I'd finished it, I still disturbed the class.

The problem was often solved by letting me go outside to work on my assignments, if the weather permitted. I especially enjoyed that. Sometimes I was given a book of poems and told to go outside to memorize a poem or two of my choice. That was not difficult because I could memorize very quickly. So I memorized many poems and had fun doing it. Memorizing other things such as the Gettysburg Address was too easy.

The teachers and school board consulted with the superintendent of schools and decided to jump me over the 7th grade and into the 8th grade. I was happy about that. Immediately several people, who evidently knew of my behavioral problems, warned me that my new teacher was known to be austere. She would not tolerate my shenanigans. So I expected this teacher to talk to me face-to-face on my first day in 8th grade.

Her reputation made me somewhat apprehensive. I'd heard that she had disciplined one of her twin brother's years earlier by making him sit on a stool in the corner, adorned with a dunce cap, until he nearly fainted. So I felt warned, "Rosalie, watch out, if she does that to her brother, just imagine what she'll do to you."

Well, our session together ended up being a stern but kind heart-to-heart talk. I had very little to say other than to answer her questions. As a result of the care she showed, my behavioral problems began to improve, at least in class. I gained much respect for her. In fact, she became my favorite teacher during my seven years of elementary school.

This teacher either liked me or felt sorry for me because on many days she would bring a sandwich for my lunch. She even purchased a class pin for me; she must have realized that I would have gone without since my family could not afford to purchase one.

To my surprise she chose me to lead the procession for our 8th grade graduation night. With that special privilege she pleaded with me to be serious and not to act up. I assured her that I would try hard, but to her it probably didn't look like I was trying very hard during our practice sessions. It was a real challenge for me to swing my baton and concentrate on keeping in time with the music as I faced the students while marching backwards. We had to march down the long hall, through a door and up stairs to the stage. In spite of my mischievousness she allowed me to lead the procession.

In those days my wardrobe was pretty slim, but on this once-in-a-lifetime occasion I had a beautiful formal dress and a pair of medium-sized heel dress shoes to wear that my dear grandmother on the mainland had purchased for me. "Wow!" I thought, "I've never dressed like this," and I wondered how I could adjust to the shoes in particular. I must have performed okay, because after the graduation service my teacher came up to me with tears in her eyes, hugged me, thanked me, and said, "I knew it, I knew that you could do it!" Many years later I would enjoy a very special visit with her. But my school career finished when I graduated from the 8th grade.

Oh, how I longed to go on to high school, but that was not to be. There was no high school on the island and I couldn't face the thought of going to the mainland to a boarding school, even if someone could afford to pay the costly board and tuition fees. Kids whose parents could afford the fees were sent there for their years of high school. Even thinking about that type of living environment brought back bad memories and put fear in my heart.

A Methodist pastor on the island, Mr. Hemming, took a

special interest in me and often did kind things for me even though I didn't attend his church or Sunday school. He knew that I liked to sketch, so when he went to the mainland he sometimes would purchase a sketch book and give it to me. It was evident that he very much wanted me to get a high school education, but could not open any doors for me to do that.

Sometime soon after leaving school I left home and lived with others working for my room and board. At different times I tried going back to live at home but it didn't work out. My stepmother and I clashed often, which was probably my fault. One day things reached a climax. Once again I was arguing with her. Then my father joined in. "I'm just sorry that I didn't do with you what I should have done sixteen years ago!" he yelled. "What's that?" I asked. "Put you in an orphanage!" was his reply. That hurt so deeply that I left home, never to return.

The rest of my experiences I'll skip out of love and respect for my stepbrother and stepsisters. We never had time to become acquainted with each other because I left home.

For some of the time I lived with my oldest brother, Ricker, and his family and other caring people. Later, I moved to the mainland and lived with an aunt and uncle and their large family. I took care of the housekeeping and cooked most of the meals during the week while my aunt and uncle went to work. After that I lived with other kind people who took me in as part of their family. I was well cared for, and in return I gladly helped them with the housekeeping and babysitting.

I am forever grateful for the kindness shown to me. I went back to Swan's Island briefly, but decided to live with other people on the mainland until I was old enough to be employed there in one of the factories.

* * * * * * * * * * * *

As for other family members, I never met either of my grandfathers. My mother's father drowned along with his son. My paternal grandfather emigrated from Sweden as a young man; he married my grandmother and they had four children.

Sometime later he decided to go to California to search for gold during the Gold Rush era. He never made it back, and as far as I know he was never found. My dad said that months later his material possessions were shipped back to his wife who was left to bring up their four children alone. I never met that grandmother either, because she lived on a larger island a good distance from where we lived.

During our childhood it seems that my three brothers, two sisters, and I fit well under the title of "The Home of the Little Wanderers." Since my brothers were older, their stay in a foster home was much shorter before they went home to Swan's Island. They were already in their late teens or older when I arrived there and met them for the first time.

My next to the oldest brother, Charles, left home shortly after I got there, so I hardly knew him until I went to live with him and his wife, Gwen, years later on the mainland. Another brother joined the US Navy. My last brother had polio as a young boy that left him partially crippled on one side, affecting the leg, arm, and hand. He always worked hard, but lobster fishing wasn't easy for him with that handicap so he went off to Connecticut in search of work, which he found. He married a girl from Connecticut and they later had three children. All my mother's children except my older, failing sister are now deceased.

Chapter 5

Freedom and Consequences

"*A*h, I'm 18 years old! Now I can search for a real job." It wasn't too difficult once I understood how to go about it.

In the beginning my "real" job experience was working in fish factories filleting fish, which I did with speed. After that I worked in different factories packing sardines in little tin containers. Sometime later I was able to start my first steady and longer-lasting job in a robe factory where they also specialized in producing dinner jackets and robes of different varieties for boxers and other famous people. I was told that they had even made the robe for the famous prize fighter, Joe Lewis.

My job was to do what I would call the first inspection. We gals cut and trimmed the threads from work that came from the sewers. A good number of ladies and girls were lined up at a long table where we stood and snipped away all day. It was hard for me to stand still but I liked the money so I kept at it without complaining. I was able to move around and do a few other things, like entertain the girls when the opportunity arose.

During my first years on the mainland I lived with several different people. Once again for awhile I stayed with my brother, Charles, and his wife, Gwen, who were kind to me even though I'm sure I was a challenge to them, especially when I was drinking. For brief periods of time I moved in with my grandmother and step grandfather. He, like my brother, was a fisherman who was gone for ten to fourteen days at a time on a deep-sea fishing trawler.

Although she never told me, I sensed that my grandmother really did love me because of the kind way she treated me. She would often embarrass me when she'd tell others, in my presence, how after my mother passed away I'd run to her in tears with my arms stretched out and in my limited baby vocabulary say, "Mama, taka me."

She had been through a lot in life. As a young woman she nearly died with rheumatic fever followed by typhoid fever, which caused her to lose all of her body hair. She wore a wig the rest of her life. Two husbands had suffered tragic deaths; her daughter—my mother—had also passed away. When she spoke of my mother's death at such a young age, leaving behind her seven children, I sensed her deep love. She knew that my siblings and I would have to be taken from the temporary homes around the island where we'd been living and be placed into foster homes on the mainland.

Now that I was grown up, so I thought, I made new friends who usually were much older than me. My lifestyle and habits changed rather rapidly. Boys, drinking, and partying soon became the pattern. Good times seemed to compensate for my inferiority complex. People evidently liked me, but I found it hard to believe! Some people wanted me to be around them, but I'm sure there were others who wished I'd get lost. My silliness sometimes would go too far...and sometimes still does! I must have been born with an ability to entertain people because I never lacked for invitations to go places. Sometimes I would stay out nearly all night, but I never missed work, nor did it affect my work.

One day I was in the home of a special friend drinking and visiting with everyone there when our fun was interrupted by tragic news. A dear friend had been washed overboard from the fishing trawler that he had shipped out on earlier that day. That news hit me especially hard because I was the one who had driven him to the wharf. As he walked away, he had said, "You take care of yourself." I had replied, "You take care of yourself because you are the one who is going out to sea."

That trawler typically had a crew of eight to twelve men on board. It would take them to the Bay of Fundy fishing grounds off the Canadian coast or to the Gulf of Saint Lawrence. After hearing the sad news, I borrowed my friend's brand-new Buick and headed to the nearby convenience store to buy more beer so we could drown our sorrows.

Very soon after driving down the hill onto the main street, I sideswiped a parked car but I kept on going, probably thinking it was no big deal. Soon after that I turned into the driveway under the canopy of the gas station pumps, but instead of hitting the brakes I pushed hard on the gas pedal. The car crashed through the large storefront window. I nonchalantly got out of the car and walked into the store, intent on buying beer. That alone was a no-no as I was not yet 21. It turns out I was already considered intoxicated. The earlier drinking had clearly affected my thinking rather quickly!

The store owner knew me because I often stopped there. "Lady," he shouted, "you stay right here while I call the police!" My sassy reply was, "Call the sheriff while you're at it!" So, while he was calling the police, I decided to leave. "Come back here, come back here!" he shouted. "Relax," I yelled back, "I'm only going to get my purse." Instead, I backed the car up and took off in a hurry and headed back to the house. I said nothing to anyone there and continued to drink. Evidently I didn't think it was serious enough, but I soon found out differently.

Sometime later there was a knock on the door. It was the policeman whom I happened to know because I had worked with his wife in the fish factory. I smart-talked to him and even offered him a drink, but that didn't help. "I hate to do this to you," he said, "but I have to serve you with these papers, and you'll need to be in court at 10:00 a.m. tomorrow."

Next morning was Saturday and I appeared in court. Of course I was sober and I was ashamed of myself, but it didn't help. Nervously I stood before the judge and denied that I was drunk when the incident happened. I explained that the drinking must have caught up with me after I arrived back at the house.

After hearing my case, the judge told me that due to lack of evidence, I would only be ordered to turn in my driver's license and pay my fine. It was around $70. I didn't have it at the time. It was Saturday morning and the banks weren't open. So I had no other choice but to go to jail. My oldest sister left in a hurry to find someone who could loan her money to pay for my fine. Meanwhile, I didn't like being in the jail, especially with the man in the cell across from me staring at me. A few hours later my sister arrived with money that someone had given her to pay my fine, so I was released. How I hated myself for the shameful behavior, knowing my grandmother had heard about it.

No matter how hard I tried, I just couldn't seem to break away from drinking with my friends, boyfriends, and others. More than once I wished I could die. When my girlfriend decided to move away to a larger city to find work and to get away from her abusive boyfriend, I decided to run off with her. But it didn't help because in the new city of Portland, Maine, I quickly made friends who liked to drink. So I went back to the same old vices. After awhile I decided to call my sister in Connecticut and ask if I could come live with her while I tried to find a job. She agreed.

Deep down in my heart I was determined that I was going to quit drinking. I knew it wouldn't be easy because it would mean staying home at night. When I left Maine, people told me it would be difficult, if not impossible, to find a job in Connecticut because at that time jobs weren't plentiful there. But they were wrong. After my first interview I was hired, and I held that job for a long time until I found a better paying job.

For nine weeks I didn't drink. I also took a part-time job in order to pay off the bill for car repairs back in Maine because I didn't have insurance. So working two jobs didn't give me much time to drink other than on the weekends. My daytime job as a machine operator at a collapsible aluminum tube factory meant that I had to hurry home to clean up and change into a uniform to work at the Dairy Joy as a waitress. I didn't have time to eat, so every night when there was a slow spell

I would eat a cheeseburger and a strawberry milkshake or an ice-cream sundae. I was grateful for the two men who were the owners for giving me the opportunity to make the extra money. They were pleased with my work and they seemed to like me.

One of the owners was also the chief of police of that small town. He liked my work performance and how committed I was at working two jobs, and I think he felt bad for me. One night he came in when business was slow and said, "Rosalie, I've watched your good behavior and work performance and I'd like to try to help you to get your State of Maine driver's license back. Would you like me to write a letter to the authorities concerning that?" "Yes!" was my quick reply. Soon after that he handed me his official letter.

I soon called a lawyer in the town where I had previously lived in Maine and he agreed to take care of that for me. I was issued a "pink" driver's license that I think was good for a year. After a period of time I was able to get a proper Connecticut Operator's license. At that point I didn't have a vehicle, but friends let me use their vehicles for errands; at other times I needed to use a taxi. I finished paying off my debt for the charges of the damaged properties back in Maine. Soon after that I purchased a used car. It was a great feeling to be debt free except for the car payments.

Chapter 6

Is Life Really Worth Living?

I often thought, "It will be great when I can finally be free from my debts and I can go buy things that I've always wanted—like a newer car, maybe even a convertible." So you can imagine how cool it was when I was able to purchase my 1958 black Mercury Monterey convertible. For a while the payments were difficult to make, so I applied for another job and was hired immediately. It was short-lived, however. Since I was one of the newest workers when this company down-sized, I was one of the first to go. Soon after that I went across the highway to a competing paper box factory, and I got a job working on the day shift.

I did the "stacker" job on a paper box folding machine. Each order varied in size and in quantity. The boxes would come from the folding machine down the conveyor belt and stacked themselves in a fan-like position. We had to quickly count them by threes and pack them into a large corrugated box. If we were too slow, we'd have a pileup and have to shut the conveyor belt down. We tried to avoid this. It was a challenge I liked because I was fast, even though at times my fingers couldn't keep up counting at the speed the boxes were coming down. I was never reprimanded, so I assumed I did okay.

At that time I weighed just over 100 pounds. I was already thin as a result of smoking two to three packs of cigarettes each day, drinking heavily, and eating poorly. Running back and forth at work really kept my weight down too. At that time I was on piecework at night and making almost double the pay, but I soon learned that money doesn't bring happiness. Instead, I battled thoughts of despair. My relationships, my heartaches, and my poor health left me even more discouraged.

At this point I was so ashamed of the choices I had made that I decided to end my life. I strongly considered buying a gun and shooting myself, but I lost courage. Next, I considered swallowing a bottle of pain pills; once again due to lack of courage I changed my mind. I knew of people who had tried that option and ended up with undesirable results that they had to live with. Somehow these people and situations interrupted my suicidal thoughts for a time. But deep down I still hated myself and life.

Drinking did give me a false sense of happiness for a little while. Later, it increased my hatred for life and the unhappiness it caused. In spite of my efforts I could not overcome these bad habits. The people I hung out with had too much negative influence on me. I felt trapped and hopeless.

Sometime around late August of 1961 I left my apartment on a Sunday night, got in my car, and headed toward the Gold Star Memorial Bridge in New London-Groton, Connecticut. Several people had jumped off this bridge and successfully ended their lives. Earlier, I had consumed a few alcoholic drinks which seemed to give me the courage that I needed. While traveling toward the bridge, I turned on my car radio to search for popular music when Billy Graham's voice came on, blasting loud and clear. Strangely, I didn't turn the dial but continued to listen. For the life of me I can't remember what his message was about. But he fascinated me. I changed my mind about jumping off the bridge, took the exit just before the bridge, and drove home.

Here's a little background you need to know. When I lived in Maine I'd often listened to Billy Graham at drinking parties. If it was on a Sunday night when I was looking for music on the radio, his preaching would often come on. Of course I really wasn't interested in his message, but sad to say I used it as a way to entertain everybody. They would laugh at me while I imitated his preaching. What a "sick head" I must have been! My lifestyle did not change, nor did my unhappiness subside.

Not long after my attempt to commit suicide, I purchased a brand-new 1961 Chevrolet Impala super sports car. In fact, it was the showroom display model—a special model to celebrate Chevrolet's golden anniversary.

At first the salespeople didn't want to sell me that particular car, but they obviously changed their minds at some point in our conversation because I drove off in a sparkling gold metallic car with yellow bucket seats adorned with a stainless steel frame. Sometime later the dealer told me that my "take off" wasn't fast enough. In their opinion I really didn't drive the car like it was made to be driven. There was no way that I was going to either, because I didn't want to get in trouble and lose my license again. Later I'll have something interesting to tell you concerning that special vehicle.

Chapter 7

Hope Is Getting Close!

*A*fter three failed attempts to end my life, I decided to try again to reform. Two close calls with my vehicle had frightened me. Besides that, I had left my car somewhere on a Saturday night and was shocked the next day when I couldn't find it. Thankfully, I had had enough sense to park it rather than drive while drinking and possibly get a ticket or endanger someone else's life.

My brother, Ricker, also caught my attention. At work one day he was electrocuted with 46,000 volts of power going through his body. He hung on the power pole for a long time until help arrived. Soon after his accident my other brother and I made a hurried trip from Connecticut to see him in the Bar Harbor, Maine hospital. I was impressed with his changed life and his testimony of Christ as his Savior. Even though I didn't want anything to do with his Jesus, I couldn't deny that he was a changed man. It left a lasting impression on me.

A year or two later I drove to Swan's Island from Connecticut, but I felt uneasy when Ricker approached me waving his one arm with a deformed hand. My first thoughts were, "He is coming to preach to me." I wasn't interested in hearing about his Jesus, and I wasn't shy about letting him know it. "Don't preach at me," I warned him. He told me that he was praying for me. I knew that he and his wife, Beulah, and other Christians on the island were praying for me, too. In fact, two ladies had prayed for me from the time I had arrived there to live. They showed me love and kindness that I'd never known, and I didn't quite know how to handle it.

God kept bringing me in contact with such people, and it concerned me deeply, so one weekend shortly after my birthday in September 1961, I decided to stay home and not drink. I had already told the girls at work, "Please don't call me or come to my house because I'm going to try to quit drinking." "What a joke!" they thought. They didn't believe it was possible, and I wasn't sure either, but I was going to try. However, I found in my cupboard a bottle of whiskey that the girls had given me for my birthday. You guessed it! I got into the bottle.

As I was sitting there alone that evening listening to long playing music records, I decided to find something else on the radio. Would you believe it—Billy Graham was on again? I listened to him, but only half-heartedly, until something he said caught my attention. It went something like this: "You may have hated yourself and you may have been hated by others, but God loves you and **He can change you**."

That last part really got my attention because that's what I was trying to do—change myself! All my efforts were unsuccessful. At the end of his preaching he offered his popular book *Peace with God*. Somewhere in my foggy mind I decided, "I want to get this book." Tears came to my eyes as I scribbled a note to him on a small piece of scrap paper. I wrote something like this:

Dear Mr. Graham,
I need help with drinking, swearing, and smoking, etc.
A sinner,
Rosalie Ranquist
P.S. Please send me your book, Peace with God.

Along with the note I also wrote a check for a small amount.

After drinking my whiskey, I went to bed. The next morning I was up getting ready for work when I noticed that letter and check lying on a small table. Being curious I read it again.

It left me feeling disgusted and embarrassed at what I had written. To make it worse, I thought "I'm wasting my money." For awhile I argued back and forth with myself about whether or not to send it. Finally, I decided it wouldn't hurt to send it; besides, the money could help them. So I headed off for work with the letter.

Just before I hit the freeway to drive twenty miles to work, I stopped and mailed the letter to the Billy Graham headquarters in Minneapolis, Minnesota. A few unbelievably short days later I was surprised to find a package in my mailbox from the Billy Graham headquarters. It seemed to have come, as the saying goes, "on angels' wings." I was baffled at how my letter had reached them so quickly. I was just as baffled by how quickly I received his book and a booklet. I thought, "Wow! Someone must really want me to read this."

Once I started to read the book, I couldn't lay it down. It began to answer the all-important question that I had wondered about all my life: "Why am I here on this earth?"

But before I go on, I need to mention another book.

While I was trying to reform several months earlier, I was also fixing up my apartment. "The coffee table in front of the sofa needs a Bible on it," I thought. "A nice new Bible would look good right here." A few days later there was a knock on my door. I found a man standing there with a smile on his face. He said something like this, "Ma'am, I would like to show you a fine line of Bibles that I'm selling today." I looked at him with surprise, and said, "You're selling Bibles?" "Yes ma'am, I have one that I'd like to show you."

So I invited him to come in. He showed me a huge, beautiful Bible with the face of Jesus in the center of the front cover. "Wow! That's just what I wanted!" With it would come another book that had all the sayings of Jesus in the New Testament. The transaction was made and for the first time ever that I remember, I owned a Bible.

During my early years in the foster home when we attended Sunday school, I can remember memorizing Scripture and hearing that everyone is considered a sinner, Jesus Christ,

God's Son, died on the cross to pay the price for peoples' sins. It was fixed in my mind that He was crucified and shed His blood. He was buried, and on the third day He arose from the grave. I knew the facts in my head. Evidently it stuck with me because of my photographic memory, but I still didn't understand it.

The book *Peace with God* and the booklet "How to Live a Happy Christian Life" helped me to understand that I was a sinner and why I did sinful things. Somehow I thought that God loved me before, but now that I was so bad He couldn't love me. Of course, I never asked anybody questions about the Bible. I thought they knew what it said, and because of that I didn't want to show my ignorance. But I learned from this book that they, too, were sinners and needed to be born again into the family of God. The whole human race needs a Savior, just like I did.

What a revelation to this messed up young woman! God was creating in my heart a desire to have a relationship with Him, but I was still worrying about my past and still trying to reform. Try as I could, I was unsuccessful. Billy Graham's book showed me that I could simply accept Jesus Christ as my personal Savior. He would cleanse me from all my sins and make me a new person in Christ. Wow!

Because I already had my new Bible, I was able to look up verses. The book told me simply and clearly about my standing with God and of God's remedy for sin. Being under deep conviction, I was determined to reform. In other words, I was going to clean myself up and then accept Jesus Christ as my Savior. Somehow my mind could not grasp the fact that God was the only One who could clean me up.

So for three or four weeks I tried to stay out of trouble, but I couldn't. I reverted to my old ways, but my mind couldn't rest.

I read *Peace with God* through several times. I even took it to work to read during break times. It wouldn't be smart to take it into the ladies' room because the girls would go into hysterics if they saw me reading it. So for part of the break time, I decided to stay behind the conveyor belt. One time the girls noticed me there and wanted to see what I was reading. So I lifted it up and showed them the cover with a picture of young Billy Graham waving the Bible. They were shocked, to say the least.

While this was all going on in my mind, I was thinking ahead because I wanted to find a good church before I became a Christian. A friend tried talking me into going to her church. I refused and went to a different one, but I wasn't impressed. During the service, I had picked up a card from the back of the pew and wrote on it that I would like a visit from the pastor. I also had some money balled up in my hand to put in the offering, but I held back both the card and the offering because I didn't feel that this was where I wanted to be.

My friend suggested that I go again, so I did, but I still didn't feel comfortable there. I decided to search the news-paper and found an advertisement for a Baptist church in the nearby town close to where I was later going to live with my single brother. "Testimonies, singing, and preaching" it said. It had night services, which I thought meant it had to be a good church. I remembered on Swan's Island, and even as a child in the foster home, that most churches had night services. So Sunday night I drove to this church, but I sat on the back row because I wasn't sure whether I'd stay or leave.

Would you believe it? Three ladies stood up in front and sang the song "In times like these, you need a Savior." "Wow!" I thought, "How did they know?" The message spoke straight to my heart even though I didn't remember what it was. When the service ended, I wanted to hurry out. The pastor was standing at the doorway to shake my hand, and when he greeted me, I said, "I think I want to be a Christian." Then I ran out the door before he could talk to me.

I was still confused, thinking that I had to help God accept me. My soul's enemy didn't want me to make a life and death decision that would count for all eternity. So the war in my soul continued.

Before leaving work on a Friday in late October, I told the girls, "I'm going to become a Christian." Well, they laughed and said unkind things in a joking way. "Honey, God couldn't save you if He wanted to!" After that another one chimed in, "I'm going to sprout little white wings and fly away!" "You just wait and see," I replied. "When I come in here Monday, I'll be a Christian." "You know what, Honey? I don't believe you," was the sarcastic reply. "You'll be a girl with a hangover!" "No, I'll be a Christian," I said and left work for the weekend.

Chapter 8

A Baby Again

*M*y heart thumped loudly. My mind fought fiercely. I had determined that this was the weekend when I would accept Jesus Christ as my Savior. So I went nowhere except to church.

A battle raged in my soul throughout the Sunday morning service. I kept wrestling, feeling that somehow I needed to try harder to help God. Sunday evening came, and once again I came home from church without deciding to trust Jesus. Like I'd done before, I turned on the radio to hear Billy Graham's voice. Toward the end of his message I remember him saying, "You may never ever have another opportunity like this to accept Jesus as your Savior. Accept Him now!"

The program ended at 11 p.m. A few moments later I threw away my open pack of cigarettes. Next, I knelt by my bed. I'd mocked many pastors by imitating them praying, but I had no clue how to pray for myself. So, with a broken heart, I cried out to the Lord, "Save me, for Jesus' sake." I truly meant it from the depths of my heart.

In that moment my life changed forever. I became His child, and I had confidence that Jesus had saved me because the salesman's Bible told me so. "For God so loved the world that He gave His only begotten Son, that whosoever believeth on Him should not perish, but have everlasting life" (John 3:16).

Suddenly, I realized that I had become a baby again—a baby

in Christ. I was so happy inside even though I kept weeping. My habitual smoking, drinking, and foul language were wrong, I knew. As were lots of other things I'd done.

Somewhere along the line I'd already memorized I Corinthians 10:13 which says, "There hath no temptation taken you but such as is common to man: but God is faithful, who will not suffer you to be tempted above that ye are able; but will with the temptation also make a way to escape, that ye may be able to bear it." As I sobbed my heart out, I earnestly reminded God of this verse and begged Him to help me trust Him to change my ways. "Lord, I'm yours for the rest of my life; I only want to be what you want me to be."

I felt like the Lord was lifting my heavy burden off my shoulders as I gave Him all my bad habits. He filled my heart to overflowing. Yet the strangest thing happened as I got up from my knees and went to bed. I still kept crying, recalling all the things I had ever done as a child up to that moment. I could not sleep. At the same time my tears were mixed with the joy of knowing that God had forgiven my every sin. Then I realized that it was early next morning and I was still awake. I needed to get a few hours of sleep before heading off to work on the second shift.

Guess what concerned me? Swollen eyes! I didn't want to go to work looking half asleep with puffed up eyes from crying. As it turned out, I felt wonderful as I headed off to my work, eager to tell the girls that I was now a child of God.

My heart is thrilled over and over again as I think of Jesus and what He has done for me. I'll praise Him on earth until my life is over, and for all eternity when I behold His wondrous face!

Chapter 9

Watch Out, Here She Comes!

*T*his day is going to be exciting for me; I'm going to show the girls at work that I'm saved and that I've changed. Last night I ripped up my opened pack of cigarettes. Now I'm going to take the two unopened cartons and give them to the girls.

When I got to work, I walked up to the conveyor belt where some of the girls were chatting. Casually, I tossed the two cartons of cigarettes onto the conveyor belt next to them. "What's this all about?" they asked. "I'm a Christian and I don't need these anymore," I replied. "You can have them." They were dumbfounded! I guess since they knew me before the change in my life, they had reason to be stunned at my announcement.

"Come on now, you don't have to be fanatical!" my old friends taunted. "You just have to change a little bit." I replied, "No, I'm sold out for Jesus Christ!" After that they didn't know what to do with me. They tried to aggravate me and test me in every way they could, but the dear Lord helped me. I was so excited to be God's child; I wanted the whole world to know how much God loved them.

More than once I slipped up, but I quickly asked the Lord to forgive me for what I'd done wrong. For example, one night a girl began to sing "The Old Rugged Cross" while doing a dirty dance at the same time. She taunted me with her movements, and kept watching to see how I'd respond. Well, my old temper kicked in. I took my shoe off and threw it across

49

the conveyor belt. It nearly hit her. Immediately, the Holy Spirit convicted me. I began to cry as I walked around the conveyor belt to her and the other girls and apologized for what I had just done. I went on to tell them that I had sinned against God. These girls did not know how to handle it. They knew the old Rosalie could lose her temper if she was aggravated too much, so from time to time they tried in different ways to make me mad.

On Friday nights the girls and I often ate together. We would take turns cooking a main dish. One particular night when I had been a Christian for only a short while, one of the ladies, who was a Polish Catholic, asked me to say the blessing for the meal. She probably did so because she had seen me pray before I ate. With my overflowing heart I thanked the Lord as best as I knew how. Shortly after that, she came up to me and in her kind, soft voice said, "Would you write that prayer down for me?" I told her, "I don't remember what I said; my prayers aren't memorized. I just prayed from my thankful heart." She was a kind and sweet lady; maybe she was even searching herself. The girls gave me a hard time, but I knew they liked me. They just wished that I was the old Rosalie I used to be.

For some time I had been working on the night shift, but I decided that I wanted to go back to the day shift because it bothered me that I was missing church during prayer meetings and other weeknight specials. I just loved being in the house of God with His people. To change shifts meant my pay would be cut in half. But I didn't care. I just wanted to be in church every single time.

Having my pay cut would pose a bit of a problem because I was still paying for the Chevrolet Impala sports car. This special 1961 car was hindering me, so I decided that I would gladly give it back to the garage. I had already paid over $1,800 on the vehicle, which was quite a bit of money in those days, but I didn't care. As far as I was concerned it didn't matter. So I went to see the main guy at the garage and told him, "You can have this car back." He looked puzzled. "What are you talking about?" "I'm a Christian," I replied, "and I don't want it anymore." "Are you crazy?" he asked. "No, I'm a Christian and I don't need this anymore!" I went on to explain that cars didn't mean anything to me anymore. I also shared the Gospel of Jesus Christ with him. He really thought I had gone off the deep end. "You won't get any money back," he explained. "I don't care," I replied. Finally, after some more talking back and forth, he realized I was serious.

My next question was, "Do you have an old bomb of a car that I could buy?" Right away I could tell he felt sorry for me. He wasn't sure that I realized what I was doing. "It's really okay," I assured him. So I ended up buying an outdated model Nash Rambler. I don't remember what year it was, but it got me around for as long as I needed it. It saved me a lot of money, even though I had to make small monthly payments. The best thing about this deal was that I was able to go to church any night that something was happening there.

I definitely left the salesman with questions on his mind as I drove that old Rambler out of there with a smile on my face and with the blessing of the Lord in my heart.

Chapter 10

Feasting on God's Precious Word

Soon after I became a Christian, I decided to clean my house of my "old life" things. Getting rid of my worldly records, which consisted of about every pop recording that was available in those days, was one of the first things to go. No one told me to do that, but I couldn't see how they were going to help me grow in my spiritual walk with the Lord. They were distasteful to me now. My heart was hungry for the things of the Lord. For the same reason I definitely wanted to get rid of books that I had.

Right away I became involved with a follow-up Bible correspondence course for new Christians, which included 120 Bible verses on cards to memorize. I didn't just memorize them, I also used them in my new enthusiasm to challenge everybody I could with the fact that they needed my Savior. As best I could, I gave them the simple plan of salvation. Some didn't appreciate it, especially the guy who was a friendly co-worker and was involved in a non-Biblical organization.

One time he needed a ride somewhere after work, so I helped him out. He immediately read the large sticker on my car dashboard which said, "The Lord is my shepherd." Well, right away he asked, "Do you think that's going to help you?" I replied, "No, but Jesus is my Lord and Savior and He has already helped me, and He wants to be your Savior too." He quickly told me some of his beliefs, but I didn't listen. Instead,

I kept saying that I didn't know about those things, but I did know that the Bible says in John 3:16, "For God so loved the world, that he gave his only begotten son, that whosoever believeth in him should not perish, but have everlasting life." Things went rather quiet after that, but he did thank me for the ride. It was no surprise that next time he needed a ride, he found someone else to help him out.

Soon after becoming a born again Christian, I went to a Christian bookstore to purchase some Bible commentaries and other books to help me study God's Word. While I was there, I decided to purchase some good Christian music to replace the worldly records that I had destroyed. I really didn't know what to buy. Mahalia Jackson's record was the first one I purchased. Over and over I played the song "On That Great Getting Up Morning." It wasn't my favorite style of singing, but at that point I just loved any Christian music.

I browsed some more and chose a record by George Beverly Shea and one of Pat Boone singing Christian songs. Another record by the White Sisters later became my favorite for a special reason. I particularly liked to play Pat Boone singing "Have Thine Own Way" every night as I knelt by my bed praying. It was the prayer of my heart—that the Lord would always have His way in my life.

Trials came fast and furiously, which I expected because I had already read in the Bible that would happen. I learned rather quickly that trials help Christians grow. They prove that, in God's faithfulness, He helps us through each trial if we let Him. I knew that God was teaching me and preparing me for something ahead. It was an exciting life!

My heart was thrilled whenever I thought about the Lord, which was most of the time. I probably annoyed some Christians, but I couldn't keep from bubbling over. I wanted to share the Gospel no matter how hidden behind the scenes I would be. But it was made clear to me that I needed to get further education with an emphasis on the Bible. I soon found myself longing to be able to go to Bible school.

My pastor had learned that I had never attended high

school, so when I kept nagging him about my desire to go to Bible school, he tried to find one that would accept me. After a few attempts, Northeastern Bible College in New Jersey agreed to accept me, but with the stipulation that I would also study to get my high school diploma. I would have gladly done that, but I would also need to work to pay for my tuition, and there weren't enough hours in the day. So I gave up the idea and chose to study on my own.

After that disappointment, it wasn't long before a different opportunity opened up. Two young men and their young families had moved from San Diego, California, to start a Christian Servicemen's Center near my area in downtown New London, Connecticut. The submarine base was just across the bridge. Not long after I became a Christian, they came to the local churches to share their ministry and to seek fellowship. My church became involved, along with many other Bible churches of different denominations in the area. Some supported the ministry financially, and many people baked desserts because the sailors often bunked at the center, which meant they were fed as well.

These two young men were great Bible teachers, so I was thrilled to attend some of their Bible studies whenever I found time between my work and church. I learned so much and became very good friends with these two wonderful families—and I've stayed in contact with them all these years. I would often tell people, "Don't get me wrong and think that I am going there to meet some nice sailor boy. No, I'm going because I'm so excited about the Lord who saved my soul and changed my life. I want to learn more about Him. That's the only reason I'm going there." It was an added blessing to get their teaching messages on tape. In my spare time I could listen to them at home.

About the same time, these two Bible teachers introduced me to excellent Bible teaching tapes of other men, so I listened to those as well. Their books and Bible study helps were a tremendous blessing. As I studied the Bible doctrines, I discovered many other "nuggets" from God's Word. Studying my Father's Word was the joy of my life. Through several avenues He was giving me what was possibly the equivalent of a Bible school education. How I thank Him for that! My God proved His faithfulness to me again and again.

One day my pastor surprised me by saying, "We'd like you to teach a Sunday school class." I said, "Me teach a Sunday school class? Why! I haven't even finished reading through the Bible. I can't teach a Sunday school class." Yet the pastor and others told me that they thought I could, so I said, "I will try." And try I did! Every spare minute I had I studied, which wasn't a lot of time because I was busy already with church activities and work.

The Lord helped me and I enjoyed immensely teaching the 5th and 6th grade boys, even though they were a tremendous challenge. Because of my own experiences with behavior problems, I had a fair amount of empathy for them, but my patience sometimes grew thin. It caused me to think about my past teachers and what they endured with me in their classes.

Sometime later, the pastor and other leaders asked me to be the missionary treasurer. Well, that frightened me, and I thought, "What makes them think I can do all these things that they are asking me to do?" Once again I agreed to try, but I didn't have a clue how to do it. Although I had an unbelievable ability at math in grade school, I'd forgotten a lot. But I stuck with both these ministries until something even more challenging confronted me.

Chapter 11

My Longtime Prayer and Desire

*E*arly in 1962, as I recall, I began to pray for God to open a door for me to serve Him full-time. I noted that date beside these verses: "Delight thyself also in the LORD: and he shall give thee the desires of thine heart. Commit thy way unto the LORD; trust also in him; and he shall bring it to pass." (Psalm 37:4-5)

I nagged the Lord about this for more than two years. I also listened to the White Sisters' song, "Lord Send Me," every night while on my knees praying before going to bed. I longed to serve the Lord with all my heart. I didn't care what I did, nor did I care if my service was obscure. I did have dreams, but would they be realized?

My interest was often aroused when special speakers and missionaries spoke at our church. I'd talk with them afterward, and they'd always ask about my education and whether I'd attended college or a Bible college. Of course, I had to tell them that I didn't even have a high school education. They'd look at me so pathetically. I often thought, "They must think I'm a moron." However, God's Word encouraged me. For example, Acts 4:13 says, "Now when they saw the boldness of Peter and John, and perceived that they were unlearned and ignorant men, they marveled: and they took knowledge of them, that they had been with Jesus." I knew the Lord was teaching me, and I really wasn't dumb.

Another Bible passage that excited me about the possibility that God could use even me for His glory is 1 Corinthians 1:26-31: "For ye see your calling, brethren, how that not many wise men after the flesh, not many mighty, not many noble, are called: But God hath chosen the foolish things of the world to confound the wise; and God hath chosen the weak things of the world to confound the things which are mighty; And base things of the world, and things which are despised, hath God chosen, yea, and things which are not, to bring to nought things that are: That no flesh should glory in his presence. But of him are ye in Christ Jesus, who of God is made unto us wisdom, and righteousness, and sanctification, and redemption: That, according as it is written, he that glorieth, let him glory in the Lord."

A glimmer of possibility came when a missionary couple from the area told about how they had started a Christian radio station in a country in Africa. I mentioned to them my disappointment that there seemed to be no open door for me to serve anywhere. The couple encouraged me to contact their mission headquarters, implying that there could be an opening for me to work in the office. So I phoned the agency and they did offer me a possible position as a typist (I'd have to go for an interview). At that time I was a hunt and peck typist, and still am. Obviously that didn't work out. But I didn't give up.

Every time missionaries spoke at our church, I'd go and talk with them. But the pattern of rejection continued—it was the same response and the same funny looks on their faces. As I prayed about this each night, I continued to give my burdens to the Lord and play my favorite song, "Lord Send Me."

I must tell you about my final encounter with a special speaker. He happened to be with a group that ministered to Jewish people. Before he could ask me the usual education questions, I surprised him by saying, "I don't have a Bible school education or a high school education." I wish you could have seen the look on his face! He then asked, "What do you do here at church?" I told him that I taught Sunday school, was the missionary treasurer, and tried to help out in other areas if I could. "Why, that's wonderful," he replied. "Churches need people like you."

Well, I'm sorry to say, I lost my cool and told him, "I'm sick of hearing people like you! Why don't you say, 'If you have a college degree, if you have a Bible school education, and if you have a high school diploma, give your life to Jesus Christ for service full-time?' I don't qualify and I'm never coming again when people like you are speaking."

Judging from the look on his face, he was shocked. Nevertheless, he kept looking at me as he reached inside his suit jacket and pulled out a pen and small tablet. "I want to write down your name and address," he said. Then he told me to expect to hear from his particular mission group, and he added, "I will be writing to you." More than forty-five years have passed and I still haven't heard from him or his mission group!

In spite of being rejected, I continued to cry out to the Lord for an open door to serve Him. A cleaning girl or anything would have been okay with me. Hopefully something would change soon.

You recall the two men who had opened the Christian Servicemen's Center nearby? They tried to help me find a ministry in which to be involved. Gary Coombs and Jay Chappell suggested that I contact the Pacific Garden Mission, a Christian rescue mission in Chicago that ministered to people in need—the drunks and the homeless, and mothers with their children who needed shelter from an abusive and sometimes violent husband.

Before I could even make contact with that mission, something happened that caught my full attention. On some Saturday nights I'd been attending a gathering of eager Christians from different churches in eastern Connecticut and Rhode Island. Often there was special music and a speaker, followed by a great time of singing our favorite hymns. After the meeting we'd go into the large homestead where some folks would gather around the two pianos to sing, or we'd just sit around and chat. Many of the ladies would bake on

Saturday afternoon and bring their special treats for us all to enjoy after the "hymn sing." I just loved going there!

This particular Saturday evening two students spoke who were in training with New Tribes Mission. If I'm not mistaken, I believe they each had a college degree. One for sure was a school teacher who was planning to go to Papua New Guinea. Toward the end of their message they made very clear the need for laborers to take the Gospel to the unreached tribes around the world. My heart started to thump! Then it began to race when I heard them say something like this: "Maybe you've been told that you are too old, or that you don't have enough education, or you've been told that you have too many children. And possibly you've also been told that any health issues would make you unacceptable. Well, those things don't have to stop you from serving the Lord on the mission field."

I felt like jumping over all the seats to get down to the front to talk with these two men. But I waited until they finished, then went right to the front. I eagerly explained how I'd been praying and asking God for an open door but I was always rejected. I did not have the needed education, and my hand had a bad case of eczema from the bleach water and other harsh cleaning supplies that I had used for so long cleaning houses for people. When I showed them my bandaged hand, one of the men said, "God can handle that too!"

Both men assured me that when they returned to the missionary training center, they would let my desires be known. They'd ask for an application to be sent to me. And they assured me that the staff and students would be praying for me.

My simple belief in God's Word at last seemed to be opening doors for me to serve the Lord full-time. I couldn't sleep that night. I kept thinking and praying and praising Him! By Sunday morning I was still ecstatic and ran around telling everybody at church my exciting news. Well, the look on people's faces was as good as pouring cold water on my enthusiasm. I'm sure that these people loved me, but I guess you could say that they didn't want me to be disappointed. Even so I just kept praising the Lord and thanking Him for this possible open door.

It wasn't long before I heard from New Tribes Mission and received an application. There was no guarantee of acceptance, but I was assured that my application would be reviewed prayerfully. I had to include several character references. Whatever my pastor and the two teachers at the Christian Servicemen's Center wrote must have been good because I was accepted to begin training that fall. I was almost 30 years old, but I felt as excited as a teenager going on a first date!

Now I had something more to tell the girls at work. But, oh, the questions people had or implied concerning the possibility of me going to the mission field! I don't think anyone believed that it could actually happen. But I did, because I had been praying for nearly two and a half years for just such a door of opportunity to open.

Chapter 12

Off to Missionary Training

*I*t was August 1964 and I was excited. In a few days I would leave work and head out in my little Nash Rambler for New Tribes Mission's missionary training center in Jersey Shore, Pennsylvania.

About a week prior to my departure, I got a phone call from an acquaintance who was a student in a Bible college in New York. "Rosie," she inquired, "are you going to that New Tribes Mission School?" "Yes," I replied, "I'll be leaving shortly to begin my training." "Oh, Rosie," she quickly replied, "you shouldn't go. My roommate's father is a pastor, and he said that New Tribes Mission is not a good mission because people got killed in the jungle and they have had planes crash, and more." It was true that people had died. The first five mission-aries to Bolivia were martyred in the jungles by the people they had gone to reach. Later, a mission leader had been killed in an airplane crash. (You can read about the five martyrs in God Planted Five Seeds by Jean Dye Johnson.)

Her words annoyed me. Why would she try to discourage me when I'd clearly seen how God had finally, and miracu-lously, opened the door for me to receive missionary training? My rather emotionally-charged reply to her was, "Will you hang up that phone and stop wasting money making a long-distance call to tell me not to do God's will?" Then I added emphatically, "Thank you!" and hung up the phone. How interesting that a short time later she left that Bible college and entered New Tribes Mission, without any influence from me. Guess what? She is still serving the Lord overseas today!

Before I left town, there was little indication that my church would help me financially, even though they knew that I would not be permitted to find employment to defray my school costs. I had saved a little money but it would not last long. However, I chose to believe what Philippians chapter 4:19 tells us. When we give sacrificially of ourselves, God promises to "supply all your need according to his riches in glory by Christ Jesus." (4:19b) I wanted to learn to trust Him to take care of me.

I'll always remember the morning that I headed out on my new adventure. I had just left my apartment to go to the nearby gas station to fuel up my Rambler when a deacon from my church, who was evidently headed for my apartment, saw me and came running toward me. He flagged me down just before I drove off. He said breathlessly, "The church family wants to send you off with their blessing and with their love and prayers." Then he handed me, if I remember correctly, a $50 check. That wouldn't be much today, but it was a great help and encouragement to me then. I thanked him and went on my way rejoicing.

Others later indicated that they would try to help me as well. And help me they did! Although this amount barely paid for food and my school fees, even though the cost was at a minimum, I saw my faithful God meet my needs as only He could.

It was late afternoon when I pulled into the training center in Jersey Shore. I just had time to unload the car and get acquainted with the girls in the dorm before darkness set in. That night my adrenalin was pumping and I started to be my mischievous, silly self. I was situated on the top of one of the four bunk beds that were three bunks high. I had with me a large lantern-like emergency light that I carried in my car. Mischievous me kept turning the big red flashing light on and off because I was too excited to sleep, not realizing that it was bothering the other girls who wanted to sleep. They must have wondered how this 30-year-old was able to get into the missionary training!

Very soon I was faced with an uncomfortable decision. The mission wanted the missionary training facility to have a family-like environment. Because space was so limited in the girls' dorm, we were told that three girls would need to move to the center in Oviedo, Florida. No one wanted to go. "Yikes," I thought. "I'm afraid of snakes and bugs, and Florida has plenty of those." We girls discussed the pros and cons between ourselves but realized we probably didn't have a choice in the matter. So we decided to be willing to go if our leaders asked us to. You guessed it—the leader of the camp came by and asked me if I would go and take two other girls with me. I had already realized that I'd probably be asked. After all, I was the only one with a car.

My old Rambler faithfully took the three of us from Pennsylvania to the little town of Oviedo, Florida. We arrived around 10 or 11 o'clock at night. The camp was tucked way back off the main road and difficult to find. Driving on a soft, sandy road felt almost like driving in snow. As we got closer we could see lights. Moss was hanging from the trees, making them look and feel spooky to this northern gal. I thought, "Oh no! What have I gotten myself into?"

Jim, who was the leader of the camp, came out to greet us. He was a kind man who had served as a missionary in Bolivia. He took us to the little two-room cabin that would be our home for the next year. One room had bunk beds and a closet; the other was the kitchen and dining area. It wasn't long before I put up a large sign over the kitchen doorway that said, "Praise the LORD anyhow!"

Our little cabin was nothing fancy, but it fitted the purpose well as we trained for possibly living in a jungle later on. I loved it there! Most of all I loved the teaching and the closeness I felt with the teachers and students. We laughed, cried, and served together as we grew in the Lord and learned more about the big job that He was preparing us for. The daily chapel times encouraged my soul. I studied hard and most nights I stayed up late thanking my dear Lord for helping me.

We attended classes in personal evangelism, New

Testament church principles, understanding cultures, as well as Bible memory. All the other girls had a Bible school education and were much younger than I was. Each afternoon we had different work assignments on the property. Right away I was given the responsibility to run the training center's convenience-type store. That meant stocking the store with staples to save the students from needing to go off-campus to buy those things. Twice weekly I headed to Orlando to buy bargains and discounted canned foods. A large retail vegetable supply house allowed me to pick up day-old fruit and vegetables. This helped many of us during the hard times when we had no money. It was a fresh way of learning to share with each other.

Without a doubt, every missionary who went through the training in those days could write a book telling of how God supplied every need like He had promised, but not necessarily every want. One time when I had no money, I decided to sell my Nash Rambler cheap to a friend at church. Soon after that, a missionary lady, Marge Day, who was on her way back to Bolivia, gave me the car that she had used during her furlough. You can't tell me that God doesn't supply our needs!

On Saturdays some of us went into the surrounding communities to share the Gospel with those we met, while others taught Child Evangelism classes. I usually accompanied a girl who was a Bible school graduate and a registered nurse.

One memorable Saturday she and I went to pass out tracts, taking turns to talk with people as usual. She was rather shy, so I had to encourage her at times to speak up. On our way to the next town we saw two men fishing on the bridge. I said to her, "We should talk to them and give them a Gospel tract." So I stopped the car and reminded her that it was her turn to talk. I'll never forget what happened.

She went up to them and said something like this, "We are fishers of men." Right away I think she realized that, because she had approached two "men," she should have started in a different way. Well, I had to try very hard not to burst out laughing. The men looked at her so strangely, but she was able to control herself and go on to explain the Gospel to them. Once we got back into the car, we laughed our heads off. She was so embarrassed, and of course I had to tease her a little bit at this funny, but innocent mistake.

During those Saturday outreaches we met some wonderful people, some strange people, and some unkind people. I became friends with three wonderful families who would have an impact on my life and missionary service for many years.

After two semesters of studying hard, all the students traveled to Wisconsin to the large Awana Youth Camp where, back in those days, New Tribes Mission held their annual missionary conference. It was inspiring to hear missionaries tell their stories of what God was doing in the regions of the world where they served. I loved the singing as well as meeting students who were in different phases of missionary training at other training locations in the USA. The food was great, too! Then it was back to Florida to complete my first training phase—a jungle survival course for six weeks.

The site was located on property that belonged to a rancher, far away from everything but cattle. We had to make our own homes out of poles with palmetto leaves for grass roofing and burlap bags for the side walls. Our beds were made of woven rope attached to poles at the head and foot of the bed. Blankets and sleeping bags served as our mattresses. Meals were eaten at a table that was built around a large tree. We tied an old parachute over the top of the table and benches to protect us from the heavy rains. Meetings were held there, too; we'd add extra log benches so everyone could sit down. I had some great times. I have vivid memories of survival hikes in the hot August sun and of severe thunderstorms that wreaked havoc on our canoe trips.

What a great feeling of success I had at the end of 1965 when our class was able to go to the next phase of training—language school in Wisconsin. But first we had a few weeks to go to our home areas for a short visit.

The Lord provided for me once again in His own sweet way. A kind family from Orlando, Florida, drove me all the way to Waterford, Connecticut, right to my brother's door. Thank you! I spent most of my time in Connecticut with a quick side trip to Maine. By the way, that kind couple became my very special friends and supporters. Their daughter, after graduating from a Bible college, became a missionary with New Tribes Mission, where she, along with her two sons, is still serving the Lord.

Chapter 13

On to Language School Challenges

*T*he time spent visiting my family and friends in Maine and Connecticut seemed far too short. While in Connecticut I met up with George and Molly Burnham, a couple from England who were also students with me in missionary training. They happened to be visiting her relative close to where I was staying, so the three of us decided to rent a car together and drive to New Tribes Mission Language School in Wisconsin.

We were challenged with courses in language and culture study, phonetics, and basic Bible translation. Different tests were administered to determine our abilities to learn a language. One week we concentrated on the language of a tribal group in Brazil, which to me was enjoyable. After that we studied Japanese for a week; that too was a pleasurable experience. I thought I did fairly well, but just recently I found a report on my time in language school which only gave me a fair grade. You see, I had a photographic memory and could memorize almost anything quickly, but when I stood before the teacher, I was plagued with a mental block.

Literacy classes often involved teamwork and were a lot of fun for me. One time our team won a prize for creating the best primer. It probably helped that one of the girls was an artist, but each of us had something to contribute and we were able to work well together. Plus I seemed to have a knack for that sort of challenge.

The tests that were administered to determine whether we had the ability to be trained as linguists proved a different story. The teacher advised us not to linger at something we didn't understand but to go to the next block of questions and answer them. Right away I knew I'd have difficulty because English grammar was not my strong suit; in coastal Maine where I'm from we had our own fisherman's lingo!

Besides having a problem with test-taking, I always needed to analyze things before I could go on. So I quickly got behind on the linguistics test and sat there trying to fight back the tears. When the test was over, I took my papers to the teacher and apologized for losing my place. He could see that I was tearful and told me, "It's okay. Other students often feel the same frustration. Just be thankful that you won't be training to be a linguist." Believe me, I was!

I enjoyed the challenge of learning a language, but I wasn't sure which one I should concentrate on. Often I talked to the Lord about my desire to serve Him in the country of Colombia. I liked the idea of traveling up and down the rivers with one of our pioneer missionary ladies, but of course she had no idea of my interest. I did ask the Lord to make it clear to me if He wanted me to go somewhere else, but in the meantime, I decided to study Spanish.

From the beginning of Spanish study my focus was interrupted by students talking about the country of New Guinea. I heard about the diet of sweet potatoes; for sure that didn't appeal to me. I also had a breathing problem so I knew it would be difficult to climb up and down mountains. Then I became friends with a lady who had worked for a short time in New Guinea. Even her influence did not arouse my interest in that place.

As far as I was concerned, I was headed to Colombia. By this time I was already into my second semester of studying Spanish, and another gal and I had been asked to be co-workers. At that time I was thinking of applying for my visa for Colombia when something strange happened—suddenly, I couldn't get New Guinea out of my mind.

For two nights I lay on the top bunk with my eyes wide open. I recalled letters I'd read about the country and recent discussions I'd had. On the bottom bunk my chosen co-worker was asleep. I clearly remember praying, "Lord, I don't understand what's going on, but I can't get New Guinea out of my mind, and because of that I haven't slept much for two nights. So Lord, if this is from you and you are trying to tell me that you want me go to New Guinea instead of Colombia, will you indicate that to me by letting me go to sleep?"

Maybe it sounds like a wild story, but right after that I fell sound asleep and slept all night! To me that meant that God wanted me to serve Him in New Guinea. Wow! How was I going to tell my leaders about this almost unbelievable experience between me and the Lord?

Next day I decided to talk to the person in charge of our work detail assignments. How would he advise me? He kindly counseled me to request an opportunity to share my story during one of our daily chapel times when all the students and staff would be together. I took a deep breath and prayed for courage. This would be hard for me.

When the opportunity came, I walked to the podium with my heart racing. I began to shake so badly that I had to hang onto the podium to keep from falling over. Everyone listened attentively as I told how the Lord had answered my prayer. I noticed that some of the students shed a few tears. After I spoke, I sat down and remained silent for the rest of the chapel time.

As usual, we all headed to our mailboxes after chapel ended. Guess what I found that day? A note requesting me to meet with our leaders right after lunch. At this point I already felt tense and unsure of how they'd respond. Remember, to me it was a miracle that I was even allowed to be in the New Tribes Mission training program. Perhaps the leaders would now think that I was nuts. I had no appetite for lunch; I just wanted the meeting behind me.

With fear and trembling, I entered the room where the school staff was waiting for me. After we all sat down, they asked me to recount my story. So I reviewed all the things that were a concern to me; I also made it very clear that I really did not want to go to New Guinea, but if that's what God wanted, I would go. I also requested prayer and guidance to make the right decision. Then I waited for their response. I'll always remember how one of the leaders, who had already served as a missionary in New Guinea, responded to me. He cocked his head to the side, as was his style, and said, "You know what? I believe God wants you in New Guinea."

My immediate response was, "What do I do now because I'm studying Spanish?" "Get out of the Spanish class and go into the Melanesian Pidgin class," he said. I felt a little apprehensive because there were linguists in that group and most students in that class could already speak the language quite well. Besides, the class would soon end. It didn't matter, so I was able to get into the class, even though I didn't learn much. I would head off for the field of New Guinea knowing very little of the Melanesian Pidgin language. Once again I would have to trust the Lord to help me grasp this language—and then later to learn yet another tribal language.

Chapter 14

At Pacific Garden Mission —My Farewells

*I*t was near the end of January 1967 when I completed language school, but I stayed for a few days waiting for money so I could travel to my home church in Connecticut. In the meantime, I received an urgent phone call from a lady who had been in missionary training with me. She and her husband had left because of health reasons and had gone back to work at the Pacific Garden Mission in Chicago where they had served years earlier. Now those same health issues were causing them to leave that ministry. She was the Assistant Director of the Women and Children's Division and he worked in the Men's Division.

"Rosalie," she said, "would you please come here and take my place. I have to leave and someone is needed to do what I'm doing." She knew my background and also realized that I would be finishing language school. But my immediate response was, "No. I'm already booked to go by ship to Australia en route to New Guinea in early April. I have to go to my home church in Connecticut as well as visit my family and friends in Maine before I leave."

She wouldn't hear of it and kept begging me to come even for a short time until a long-term replacement could be found. From her point-of-view they needed someone like me because I could identify with some of the needy people. Well, that grabbed my heart, even though I was unsure that I could do what would be expected of me. After taking some time to pray and think about it, I got back to her. "Okay," I said, "I'll give you six weeks."

That would leave me only three weeks to visit my church in Connecticut and see my family in Maine before I needed to get back to Wisconsin in time to drive to California where I was to catch a passenger ship. For now, I needed a ride to the Pacific Garden Mission in Chicago as soon as possible. Since I no longer had a car, an NTM student familiar with Chicago kindly drove me to my destination.

In order to be officially accepted at the mission, I had to give my testimony to make sure of what I believed, and that I agreed with their doctrines. I must have passed the "test" because they asked me to start work as the temporary Assistant Director of the Woman's Division. This would prove to be a rewarding experience. It wasn't long before Jack Odell, the producer and director of the "Unshackled" dramatized radio program, told me that he'd like to broadcast my testimony.

At first I responded negatively. I had been asked many times to give my testimony and was a bit tired of doing so. But then Jack said, "Do you realize that God may be able to reach some souls using your life story, so why wouldn't you want Him to do this?" Of course that caused me to think. "Okay," I replied, "you can do my story, but I won't tell everything about my past life, so you'll have to read between the lines." He agreed to honor that, so we sat together for about three hours. I wept as I told my story and he took down the details in shorthand.

Two days later he had a handful of mimeographed copies ready to give to the professional actors at the theater in Chicago. It made me teary-eyed to listen and watch them, but I controlled myself as best I could. It amazed me how well these professional actors could go through a script that they had not seen before and verbally act out each person's part with the proper lingo. A few weeks later my story was heard on about 600 radio stations around the world. I trust that God has used it for His glory.

At a later time I'd be surprised to hear my "Unshackled" story in a most unexpected place. I had gone to visit a missionary couple who worked among the Elimbari people; this group bordered the Sinasina tribe where I was serving in New Guinea. "Do you know where to find the New Tribes Mission messages on shortwave radio?" my friends asked. "Yes," I replied, "I listen daily to the radio 'sked.'" In the late 1960s that was the way our mission would send important messages from the field headquarters.

So I started to fiddle with their radio, but the dial was a little different than mine. As I was hunting for the place where I thought the radio 'sked' should be, I happened to hear a familiar voice. "That's me, that's me!" I yelled. My friends thought I was crazy. After I calmed down, they began to listen. Here in the middle of nowhere my "Unshackled" testimony was being broadcast from the Philippines! It was my story.

Through the years I've learned that missionaries in Africa, Asia, and South America have heard it in some of their remote areas on Christian shortwave radio stations. An "Unshackled" worker has told me that my story has been replayed many times and they've put it in their classic files. In fact, in 2001 they upgraded it by using much of the original script and different actors. But to me the most amazing thing was to come upon the story myself on a shortwave radio in a remote tribal region in New Guinea.

I'm getting ahead of myself, so let's go back to my time in Connecticut after I left the Pacific Garden Mission. A lot needed to be accomplished in the three weeks before I'd begin my journey to New Guinea.

Up until this time I had no promised support from any church. New Tribes Mission is a faith mission, which means that each missionary is responsible to trust the Lord to meet his or her needs through churches or individuals. A team of faithful prayer partners is essential, too.

During the training phase, I was blessed to receive gifts from my home church from time to time; a few individuals also sent gifts. But now that I was heading overseas to serve, there was nothing in black and white to say that the church, or any church, was going to support me on a monthly basis. I'd heard a hint that they might possibly send $50 a month. Two individuals also told me they would like to send $10 or $15 a month as they were able. But that was all I knew. For sure, I needed to keep trusting the Lord to provide.

Soon the time came to say goodbye to my home church family. I'll never forget my commissioning service. The believers showered me with practical things that could be used on the mission field. They even had a reporter from the local newspaper take my picture and interview me. It was a very special time of encouragement.

After the evening service, we were standing around talking for the last time, when my pastor came up to discuss a couple of things with me. "Rosalie," he said, "how are you going to live?" I replied, "I'm going to live by faith." He came back with, "I know, but who?" I said, "God." Again he said, "I know, but who?" I repeated again, "God!"

At that point it dawned on me that he wanted to know what churches were going to support me. Since no churches had made commitments at that time I told him, "Pastor, I think if God sends me to some jungle, and if He doesn't give me the money I'll need to buy food, or the native people don't give me the food I need, I think He will give me the grace to die." Everything went quiet for a few seconds.

Then he asked me, "Are you going to learn another language?" "That's what they say we do," I replied. "Well, you don't even speak very good English," he said. "I know, but they tell me if you learn another language it helps you with your English," I answered. After that he indicated that the church would be praying for me, but he didn't say anything about the money side of it. I thanked him for all they had done for me, and for their love and concern, but most of all that I was grateful for their prayers. A few days later I'd be packing up and leaving for California.

Gradually my home church and several individuals would become faithful supporters in prayer and finances. People would sometimes increase the amount of their gift. At other times, that gift would diminish or the person would cease to give. The Lord would bring along other ministry partners to help provide my needs. This is typical of the life of a missionary who desires to walk by faith trusting God.

You need to know that I had a very good relationship with my pastor and his wife. While we didn't quite see eye to eye at the point of my departure, our relationship grew stronger over time. The pastor and his wife supported me for many years after they left the pastorate and moved to New York City, and later to Massachusetts where they passed away. I stayed with them during my furloughs whenever I had meetings in their home churches. They, like many other people, had just never met anyone like me, but I became one of their personal missionaries.

Chapter 15

An Unforgettable Trip
Across the USA

*F*inally the day arrived that I'd looked forward to for so long. In late March 1967, friends drove me from Connecticut to New York City to begin the first leg of my journey across the United States to San Francisco, California. Arrangements had been made for me to pick up a car at a drive-away agent. This company hired individuals to transport vehicles for owners who flew to their destination. I found myself alone in a huge, unfamiliar city, but I was eager to see the vehicle that I'd be driving to Rockford, Illinois.

Following the formalities, the dealer took me to a nearly new 1967 Oldsmobile Toronado—a beautiful, high-powered vehicle similar to a super sports car. Off I headed, but I quickly became concerned as I entered one of the tunnels. I always feel claustrophobic in closed-in areas. Believe me, I continually prayed for the Lord's help as I slowly drove through the tunnel. The traffic behind me didn't like it one bit!

I became somewhat familiar with this powerful car as I made good progress across Ohio and into Indiana. I thanked the Lord for His help and for the nice weather. Things seemed to be going really well until I got near the Illinois border.

It was late afternoon but the sky began to get dark as if night was approaching. Clouds increased and it got foggy with rain and wind. Visibility decreased dramatically as the wind gusts increased, but I didn't dare stop for fear of not being able to pull off the road far enough and getting hit.

Then a radio announcer began talking about a tornado that had gone through an area near Chicago. I must have been on the edges of it. The wind gusts were lifting my car a bit, but thankfully I was able to drive snug behind a big trailer truck that was barely moving. It protected me from some of the high wind and the tail lights guided me as we went along very slowly. Evidently the truck driver was eager to keep on going, too, so I stayed behind him until he turned off at some point. But I kept going straight ahead.

The weather began to clear, so I continued in the light rain on what appeared to be a country highway with no buildings in sight. After awhile I realized that the truck driver had probably turned off toward the Interstate highway—I should have followed him! Suddenly, I heard and felt a thump, thump. My car had a flat tire. It was dark and scary when I got out to open the trunk. The spare tire looked brand new but it was too heavy for me to lift, so I got back into the car and cried, "Lord, please protect me and guide me!" My nerves felt frayed as I sat there with the door locked and the parking lights on.

After what seemed a very long time, I saw the lights of an oncoming car. The driver pulled over and a man came up to my window that I had only opened a crack for him. He asked if he could help me. I was unsure of him because I could tell by his smell and speech that he had been drinking, but I urgently needed someone to help me. Even though I was very afraid, I felt that I had to accept his kind offer. So I got out of the car. After much difficulty he managed to get the heavy tire out of the trunk and on to the wheel. While he was putting away the flat tire, I started talking to him about the Lord; he listened and accepted some Gospel tracts. "Please read these," I urged him. He said he would and then asked me where I was going. When I told him, he looked at me and shook his head and said, "Lady, you are way out of your way. You've gone miles past the turn off."

He gave me directions for a shortcut to the Interstate, which took me through a small town late that night. As I drove slowly down the main street, I was suddenly approached by a car with three or four men inside. They came alongside, which was far too close for comfort, and kept laughing and signaling for me to pull over. Evidently they had bad motives, because they tried to force me over so I'd have to stop.

Even though I was frightened, I decided that I'd veer into them if I had to, rather than stop. Thankfully, at that point another car came along, so the guys moved over and I sped away. I felt very shaken. "Oh Lord," I prayed, "please help me. I can't take much more." But I knew deep down that He was with me through it all, and would be with me no matter what was ahead. I remembered 1 Peter 5:7 that says, "Casting all your cares upon Him, for He careth for you."

What a relief to finally turn onto the Interstate and drive up to the tollgate. But the man in the toll booth looked at me with surprise. "Lady, are you crazy? Don't you know what's happened in Chicago?" I explained that I had just recently found out about it when I ended up lost on a back highway. "A tornado has gone through parts of Chicago, and the electricity is off, and the telephone lines are down in much of this area," he said. "You shouldn't be driving out that way."

So I asked for advice. "Lady, the best thing for you to do would be to head toward O'Hare Field and find a motel there." He just shook his head in disbelief as I drove off toward the Interstate. But I had only gone a few yards when I heard and felt a thump, thump again. So I quickly stopped the car and got out to look. The spare tire had gone flat. So I walked back to the tollgate to tell my sad story to the same man.

In those days there were no cell phones, so I asked the man if he could call a garage and ask someone to come fix my tire. "Sorry, lady," he said. "There's no power so everything is closed." By then I was very tired. "Could you see if an emergency vehicle could come and help me?" I pleaded. Well, an emergency vehicle did arrive. They put air in the tire and told me to turn off the Interstate and try to get to a motel nearby.

How grateful I was for their help!

It was about 11 o'clock when I entered the motel, weary, and asked if I could have a room for the night. "Sorry, ma'am," the clerk said. "Every motel is full because of the tornado." So with great emotion I told her my story. In my earlier years I had known people who worked in motels and knew that they always had emergency rooms for their own staff. So I looked her in the eye and asked if they would have a little closet room or an emergency room that I could use. The clerk paused and sighed, and then she agreed to give me one of those rooms. I thanked her profusely and hurriedly phoned Julaine Boye, my co-worker-to-be, who lived in Wisconsin. After talking to her I took a shower and went to bed, exhausted.

Next morning, Julaine, along with her dad and sister, drove down from Wisconsin to meet me. When we went to check out the car, to my amazement the tire was fine. So I took off for Rockford, Illinois, to drop it off at the garage. It was comforting to know that my friends were following behind me all the way. What a relief to leave the drive-away car in Rockford and continue to Wisconsin with Julaine! I was my chipper self again.

While in Wisconsin, Julaine and I, visited some of the staff and students at the language school in Waukesha where we had studied. Soon after our arrival, I was walking through one of the open areas when I heard an announcement over a loudspeaker telling students to turn their radios on to hear the Rosalie Ranquist story on the "Unshackled" program. It was being broadcast on the Milwaukee Christian radio station. For a moment I wanted to go and hide. I felt embarrassed and ashamed, even though I knew that I had been cleansed and forgiven.

Julaine and I were thankful for the opportunity to say our goodbyes in person before starting on the next part of our journey to California. One of the students drove us to Chicago where we picked up our next drive-away car—a year-old 1966 Chevrolet Impala.

The trip went well until Lockwood, Nevada, when a lady sideswiped my driver's side with her pickup truck as she went speeding through a red light. This caused a day-and-a-half delay so a garage could do repairs, which put us behind schedule. Finally, we made it to a motel in Reno, Nevada, around 9 o'clock. Not long after that, Julaine began to vomit and feel terrible. She was sure she wouldn't be able to travel the next day, but I told her that we had to deliver the car to the garage south of San Francisco on time or we'd be fined. About an hour later I began to vomit and feel terrible as well. Evidently, we had food poisoning from eating at a fast food drive-in restaurant.

We prayed together and eventually went to sleep. In the morning we felt a little better, but weak. I was determined to keep going so off we went at a decent pace until we came upon snow somewhere in the mountains in California. The roads were slippery and we had to slow down. But we made it to the appointed garage in time.

Our pleasure at reaching the goal diminished somewhat when the agent who was supposed to compensate me for delivering the car to them decided not to pay me. According to him, the vehicle was still out of alignment even though the garage in Nevada claimed to have fixed it. We didn't argue but decided to press on.

Next day I rented a car and drove to Market Square in San Francisco to collect our prepaid ocean liner tickets from the agent. At the time of purchase we were guaranteed a two-berth cabin on a higher deck at dockside, which would make travel more pleasant for Julaine, who was troubled with motion sickness. To our disappointment, the agent apologized and said we'd have to wait until we arrived in Vancouver, British Columbia, before that cabin would be available. Thankfully, we would only need to spend one night on the bottom deck.

Afterward, we headed across San Francisco Bay to Oakland and the Home of Peace, where the crates and drums that we'd sent ahead of us were now stored. Our containers would travel with us as part of the ticket price. The Home of Peace was a shipping and receiving ministry for missionaries and full-time workers in the Lord's service, but it also provided a guest home that served those who were traveling to overseas ministries. It became our temporary home until we boarded ship for Australia.

While in Oakland I hurriedly wrote and sent a letter to my church, sharing all the experiences that I had encountered in my travels across America—with emphasis on God's faithfulness to care for me in each situation. I made it clear that I had complete assurance in my heart that I was in God's will, even though my trials in route might cause some to wonder.

Someone later wrote to tell me that the pastor had made copies of my letter and given them to the church congregation; he had even made mention of me and my experiences on his Sunday radio program. As a result, the people now seemed to understand that God was leading and providing for me in every way. The church family has faithfully supported me since then. What a tremendous blessing and encouragement they have been, and continue to be, after all these years!

Chapter 16

Off to Australia and New Guinea

*H*ow exciting to finally board the British HMS Arcadia ocean liner and set sail from San Francisco for Vancouver, British Columbia! Some passengers would dis-embark there and new passengers would board, which meant that Julaine and I could move to the promised two-berth cabin on an upper deck. It would be twenty-four days until we reached Sydney, Australia.

After a few days on the open waters of the Pacific, we docked in Hawaii where we spent an enjoyable day. Julaine had already started to be a little seasick, so she was glad to put her feet on solid ground. For days after, we saw only great expanses of sea and sky until we docked in Auckland, New Zealand. A Christian couple met us, fed us, took us to their church, and gave us a little tour around the outskirts of Auckland. It was their tradition to meet the passenger ships and share their hospitality with some of the passengers.

We sailed through very rough waters from New Zealand to Sydney. Poor Julaine was seasick most of the way. Even the medicine that she had brought with her didn't seem to help. Without her knowing it, and to her displeasure, I went to the doctor on board to ask for medicine, or for him to check on her. He did what he could and it helped a little, but we both were glad to disembark. A leader from the New Tribes Missionary Training Institute north of Sydney met us at the dock and helped us through the formalities of obtaining our crates and drums that contained supplies for our ministry in New Guinea. From there he drove us to the mission headquarters where we stayed for a few days before flying to New Guinea.

I was surprised when the mission leader asked me to give my testimony at the church service that Sunday evening. It made me very nervous, but as always the dear Lord helped me tell my story. Perhaps the "Aussies" understood my speech better than some in America because they pronounce words with an "r" in the middle or at the end, the same as I do. Maybe I should say "somewhat" the same, because they do have their own unique accent.

Visiting the local area and meeting some of the students and staff was a great help to me. I learned their expressions and customs at mealtime. I also learned that it's quite chilly at night in early May and there was no central heating in our little guest apartment. So I solved the problem by taking out a hot water bottle that I'd packed to use at night in the Highlands of New Guinea. The next morning one of the ladies kindly asked if we'd like a cup of tea. I blurted out that I'd already made coffee with water from my hot water bottle. She looked at me as if to say, "Is she crazy? Is this gal for real?" That was my first blunder. I had to learn the hard way, but when I left we all were friends.

Once we finally reached New Guinea, it was necessary to stay on the coast in the capital city of Port Moresby for a few days. There we applied for work permits and other required papers. We felt at ease in a private missionary guest house with people who loved our Lord. After our business was finished, we flew to Lae, another coastal town, before changing planes to fly to Bulolo, a small town where the gold miners' years earlier bought their supplies before moving into their camp in the Watut Valley. Our first NTM missionaries in New Guinea had established a support center in that area, and from there they could move into other tribal villages to serve.

Our stay in the Watut tribe would be brief but exciting.

On the first night we visited two single missionary ladies who were serving there. They didn't have electricity. Their living room had dark wood walls, and while we were sitting there a large spider came down in front of my face. I jumped out of my chair screeching and about went berserk! What an awkward introduction to missionary life. I quickly learned that Ruthie was a practical joker, like you know who! She'd used an artificial bug, but it looked very real in that dimly lit room. More traumatic experiences were ahead.

One of the missionaries at the center was a Bible teacher and a dentist. He was also a medic who cared for some of the needs of the tribal people who came from villages near and far for medicine. One day he sent word asking me to come to the clinic where two people had arrived with suspected Death Adder snake bites. He thought I would benefit from observing the procedures that he and his wife were using to prevent possible death. At the same time he assured me that I would probably never experience such incidents in the higher altitude area where I would be working, but it still gave me a creepy feeling to observe the situation.

On another night I went to the outside toilet in the dark, taking with me a flashlight, of course. Just as I was about to open the door, the flashlight shone on a Death Adder snake to the right of the door. I let out another deathly screech and started to run back to the house as fast as I could. Believe me; I was ready to go to the Highlands. It was clear to me that God was teaching me to trust Him with the things I feared the most.

From the Watut Valley we traveled up to the Highlands regional headquarters which was then located in the Yagaria tribe. The school for missionary children was also there, and this is where Julaine and I would receive orientation in preparation for moving into a tribe.

We arrived during the annual field conference when all the missionaries had come from various tribal locations for refreshment and encouragement. Guest speakers and missionaries gave challenging messages, and there was plenty of time to become acquainted with missionaries who were involved in the rigorous discipline of learning a tribal language and culture from scratch. Others were involved in church planting; their reports of how God was changing tribal people's lives for His glory encouraged us all. One area that spoke most to me was the need to pray—especially for one another if we really wanted God to do a great work in the lives of the people that we hoped to reach with the Good News of Jesus Christ.

After consulting with Julaine and me, the field leaders decided that she and I would join the team that was working in the Sinasina tribe. Chuck and Wanda Turner had established the work and were translating the New Testament into the tribal language; Ben and Bonnie Kulp along with Nell Dreghorn, a widow from Australia were also part of the team. In preparation for our arrival, they had put up a simple bush guest house where we'd live for almost a year until we could build a more solid home.

How grateful we were for that small two-room house with bamboo floors. The walls were made of woven, cane-type materials. Our shower stall was made of sheets of thin, flat iron, with a plastic shower curtain pulled across the front and around part of the sides. It had flat iron on top of the bamboo for the shower floor. The shower fixture was a galvanized bucket with a sprinkler-type nozzle screwed into the bottom of the bucket; you stood underneath it and turned the nozzle on and off so the water could spray on you. Our wood stove served us well for cooking and for heating the house during the cool, early mornings and late evenings. The house had only three windows made of heavy plastic, but I was able to add more soon after we moved in. I used some of our crate boxes to make bottom kitchen cupboards. We hung a piece of cloth over a metal wire to cover the open front of the cupboard and to ward off bugs, as well as the stares from our tribal visitors.

We soon got into a somewhat routine schedule of studying the culture and language. Chuck Turner had translated twenty-seven language lessons into the Sinasina dialect for us. This was a boost to me, because I was limited in trying to communicate with the people in the trade language, Melanesian Pidgin English. I knew a small amount, whereas Julaine was competent in it. I had been able to communicate with the people using hand signs and facial expressions, but of course that wouldn't work if I was trying to share the Gospel with them. Once again my photographic memory aided me as I quickly memorized all the Sinasina language lessons. Soon I was able to communicate quite well in everyday conversations, but it would take more time to learn spiritual vocabulary and know how to use it appropriately.

Several times a week Julaine and I hiked to different villages to hold literacy classes, which took the better part of our mornings. Each afternoon our team spent time in prayer; then we studied the language for the rest of the afternoon as well as some evenings. That was our schedule until we moved into a bush house that we had built right in the middle of the village. In that location we got more exposure to the culture and became more fluent in the language. We had lots of fun as we worked together, played together, ate together, and laughed together with the Sinasina people. Later, we would relish the opportunities to talk with the people about the Lord and His Word.

The village people made us feel accepted and the head man of the village and his wife became our "papa" and "mama." They were responsible for our well-being. Whenever tribal fighting broke out, they would send us back to the Sinasina mission center if the fighting came too close. My tribal mama is still living today, but very old and feeble.

Earlier in my story I mentioned a toboggan injury that had left me with a breathing problem. It had never been corrected, so I could only breathe through one side of my nose—pinhole breathing, it was called. Hiking up and down the mountains to various villages meant that I kept breathing through my throat. This caused sore throats as well as infected throats and led to my having to take antibiotics far too often.

In connection to this an interesting thing happened. Someone from my church wrote to ask if I needed a vehicle.

I replied that I thought it would be great because hiking was difficult for me because of my breathing problems, but I didn't know if that's what God wanted. Besides, I had no money to buy a vehicle. Shortly after that I met one of our missionaries who was planning to sell his four-wheel-drive Jeep hard top, because his family was returning to the states. Jokingly he asked me if I wanted to buy it. Of course I laughed and said with a grin, "I'd love to have it, but I don't have any money."

To my surprise, not long after that conversation my monthly allowance statement came and on it was listed a $1,000 gift for me from someone who had never sent gifts to me directly; she had always given through the church missionary fund. Was that a coincidence? No, I don't think so! This lady was a widow with limited funds, but she was a very dear friend. She had sent the gift to me in memory of her son who was killed in Vietnam. Evidently, it was part of the insurance payment that the government pays to those who have lost a loved one in time of war. I know that only God could have orchestrated that and met my need according to His promise in Philippians 4:19 once again.

Chapter 17

Early Years Overseas

*J*ulaine and I continued with our village literacy classes and grew to love our students. Some of the older ones struggled with learning to read because of poor eyesight; it was also difficult for them to think outside of their culture. Learning to hold a pencil and write at the same time was a challenge, while some had a hard time holding the book right side up. They were almost like preschoolers. Many eventually learned the skills with extra tutoring, while other older students found learning too hard, especially with garden work and other daily responsibilities; but most agreed they enjoyed the experience of trying. Many children and young adults became good readers.

At night we'd sit around the fire until bedtime in the large men's house, which was a communal gathering place. Most of the villagers sat around the smoky fires to discuss the day's business—usually related to their pigs and gardens, which for them was the essence of life. Julaine and I listened carefully to the chatter, and after the serious talk was over the people were always willing to converse with us.

They'd often ask Julaine and me to tell them stories about America and our families. Of course, they loved to tell us their stories, too. And we always wanted to hear them, because it was another way to sharpen our language and culture knowledge, which was so important if we were going to have a ministry with them.

We often ate with the villagers, especially with our tribal mother and father and other family members. One evening as we were sitting around the fire eating, I kept talking because I was eager to use the tribal language. My very serious tribal father didn't like me to ask him questions, so he shouted at me in Sinasina, "Will you shut your mouth! Don't you know we don't talk while we are eating?" I replied, "Oh Father, I'm sorry," and shut my mouth. Usually they were helpful to answer my questions at any other time.

It was a joy for Julaine and me to see most of our clan brothers and sisters as well as some of our literacy students come to know Jesus Christ as their personal Savior. But in later years we were saddened to learn that some were not following the Lord. The white man's culture was fast moving in upon them, bringing with it the traps of gambling and alcohol.

What a blessing it was to have a four-wheel drive Jeep to get around to most of the villages, or at least to get much closer to them. My clan brother, Josia, often traveled back and forth with me to the other villages and to our main center. It was important to have someone with me in case I had trouble with the Jeep.

One time I had to go to the coastal town of Lae, which in those days was about an eight-hour drive on a dusty road full of ruts. Josia and I were making steady progress, and were glad when we got over the mountains safely and into the valley where the road was quite straight. It still looked and felt like we were driving over furrows in a garden in some places.

It was very hot in the lowlands and since we had no air conditioning, we had the windows rolled down. We drove fast in order to skip over the bumps, which kicked up a lot of dust. By the time we reached our destination, we would have reddish-white colored hair and eyelashes, as well as dust all over our faces and inside the Jeep.

That lowland stretch, I believe, was about sixty miles. Somewhere down the road the vehicle just stopped. Josia became fearful because he knew that the tribal people in that area were known to be deep into a Satanic-type religion; they practiced witchcraft. Other tribes often feared them if they wandered into their territory. Josia was afraid. There seemed to be only two options: either I would have to leave him there to watch out for the vehicle while I went to the town, or I'd have to stay there with the vehicle and send him to town for help.

We prayed together and asked God to help us get the Jeep started or to bring someone along who would help us. Some cars went by, but they seemed to be going too fast to stop. So I got out of the Jeep and started shaking and rattling things under the hood. Amazingly enough, I got back into the Jeep and it started! Josia and I began to praise the Lord with great thanksgiving as we traveled toward our destination.

Sometime later we drove into our mission guesthouse facility in Lae and parked the Jeep, when suddenly we saw smoke come rolling out from under the hood. "Wow!" was all that we could say as we jumped out. Evidently the wiring was the problem. God had protected us in a wonderful way. The Jeep was taken to a garage where it was repaired for our trip back, which was a common occurrence each time we drove to Lae on those rough roads. Josia and I purchased the necessary items for everyone before heading back to the Highlands. We felt a little apprehensive about the journey because the rough roads would take a toll on us and the vehicle. But once again we thanked God when we reached our village home safely.

In 1971, after a busy first term in the Sinasina tribe learning the culture and language and teaching literacy, it was time for our first furlough. Julaine and I packed up our house and pre-pared for our trip to the USA. The things I was taking along had to be packed securely in a plywood crate. I started to do paperwork before we departed for Australia. From there I would travel on the ocean liner HMS Australias, and arrive 24 days later in America. Julaine would fly home because of her problem with sea sickness. In those days it was still cheaper to travel by ship. Because of the free baggage allowance, I was able to take along a large box of artifacts and books to use in my meetings during furlough.

On board the vessel I met a fine Christian couple; we stuck

together and became very special friends. We enjoyed stopping in New Zealand and the Fiji Islands, where we spent the day, and I was able to bargain for a slide projector to use in meetings that I hoped to have. From there we went ashore in Acapulco, Mexico and Panama City before finally sailing through the Panama Canal and on to Fort Lauderdale, Florida.

Just prior to leaving the ship, I collected my mail at the ship's office and found a memo from the treasurer of my home church in Connecticut. The abbreviated message said: "Don't do anything about purchasing a car before you call me." Well, at that time I didn't even have enough money to get to Connecticut, let alone buy a car. Because I was to speak at a meeting in Florida and two or three in Tennessee, there was a possibility that the Lord would provide me enough funds to get to my brother's home in Connecticut.

A fellow missionary on furlough from Brazil lived in the Fort Lauderdale area, so he met me at the dock and took me to his home where I could stay until I could make arrangements to travel north. He was driving a Pontiac Tempest station wagon; with the back seat pulled down my crate of artifacts and books fit perfectly. As we conversed he asked, "Do you want to buy this station wagon?" I laughed and said, "Yeah, I'd love to, but I don't have any money to buy a vehicle." But I did ask him the cost. "I'd like to get $1,000 for it," he replied. Wow, that was something to dream about, but I still needed to call the treasurer at my home church. When I did, I learned that they had been looking for a furlough vehicle for me but had decided it would be better for me to find what would best suit my travels.

It's always been difficult for me to ask for money even when I've needed it, but this time I decided to ask him the amount that they had in mind—maybe $400 to $600? "The church has decided to give you $1,000 for a vehicle," was his reply—the exact amount that my missionary friend had in mind for his vehicle. How excited I was to purchase this station wagon that the church knew nothing about, yet it was just what I needed for my crate and luggage to fit in the back, and the price was right!

For quite some time I had not felt well. Some weeks later tests were done that showed that I had a bad case of amoeba. That condition along with my fears of having to speak at meetings was not a good mix.

My main fear of speaking stemmed from what my pastor had said to me just before I left for my first overseas assignment. His words kept coming back to my mind: "You don't even speak good English." My first meeting was scheduled for a small church in Florida where I had attended in 1964 during much of my missionary training time. By now they had a new pastor, who, unknown to him, was about to give me a boost for future meetings.

He caught my attention when he said "I has did" within a sentence. It was probably a mistake on his part but God used it to encourage me. If that pastor could make such a grammatical mistake, there was hope for me. So when I got to the much larger church in Tennessee, I told them about my fears because of what I'd been told concerning my poor English. I explained how a pastor in Florida who had been to a Bible college and seminary had encouraged me with his mistake. If he could say "I has did", then I felt that I would manage okay by using the best grammar that I knew. Well, that proved to be a huge icebreaker! From then on God always gave me the words to say as I spoke straight from my heart.

Through contacts of friends in Tennessee, God gave me other opportunities to speak, mainly to Sunday school classes. It was wonderful to finally arrive in Connecticut to be with my home church family. They had supported me faithfully during my first term and, I should add, have done so ever since.

While there, my brother Carlton and his wife, Maureen, kindly let me stay with them. Off I'd go on a variety of speaking engagements to the mission's training centers, to churches, or to share with people in their homes. I also taught a Sunday school class in my home church. Joyce Van Ness, a wonderful young lady at church, helped me each time, and then substituted for me when I was traveling. Opportunities to tell of my experiences in New Guinea increased as friends, or friends of friends, or others who had heard my story on the "Unshackled" radio program in their area, invited me to do so. But I knew that the opportunities were really from God.

This continued in my home state of Maine, where many people became acquainted with me for the first time. As a result, some started to send me small, but regular ministry support, which was a tremendous encouragement. Of course, it was good to see my family again as well as dear friends that I'd known through the years. I also made it a point to visit my 8th grade school teacher—the lady who had taken a special interest in me in my last year of school.

Now she was much older and sickly, but her face lit up with joy when I surprised her by walking into her home. During our conversation, I told her about the work I was doing in New Guinea. Then I saw her eyes fill with tears as she said, "I knew it! I knew it! You've got it! You've got it!" As I looked at her with a smile on my face, I said, "You can have it too," and went on to share the good news of the Gospel of Jesus Christ with her. I have no evidence that she trusted the Lord Jesus as her Savior, but I hope I'm wrong and that I will see her in Heaven one day.

Chapter 18

Abundant Guidance and Provision

*C*hanges came quickly during my next few years over-seas. To begin with, the country of New Guinea had become independent so it was now Papua New Guinea (PNG). Julaine and I were in our former village for a brief time when we had to make some choices concerning our lit-eracy program. Christians in the village of Duu Sinma, a few miles away, knew what we were doing, so the village leader requested us to come and start a literacy school. The Lord led me to go to that village where many learned to read and write the Sinasina language. Julaine moved to another small village, where the people had very little interaction with our missionaries; she began to establish relationships and also taught literacy to a small group.

The work in Duu Sinma progressed well, but something began to weigh heavily on me. For a long time I had been con-cerned about the people in the Gunange area, a hard-to-get-to place where the people spoke another dialect of the Sinasina language. Now I found myself frequently asking God to please send a man to that area so the people could have an oppor-tunity to hear the uncorrupted Good News of Jesus Christ. Up until then, there was no one available to go.

Well, to my amazement, one day I answered a knock on

my door to find a man standing there with a handwritten note from the village chief council member, who was the leader of that area. Translated into the trade language, the note said that there were thirty-six people who wanted to learn to read and write in their own language. "Would you come and start a school in our village?" the note said. This wasn't the answer to my prayer that I expected, but I ended up moving to that remote area of the tribe after I finished in the village of Duu Sinma.

In time I had a bush house built on tall posts, which the local men cut from their limited supply of trees. They also wove the small bamboo for the siding and for the wall divider to close off my sleeping den from the small kitchen—yes, it was small. After all, I'd only stay there for a short time, because my ministry took me back and forth to various locations. The roof was made of grass with two pieces of corrugated iron on one corner to catch rain water for drinking. There were no inside toilet facilities, which was the same in every village where I lived. My shower was what I called a "Micky Mouse" job and wobbly. I did the inside work myself since no one was available to help. This meant I made my own rough furniture. When I wasn't eating food with the people, I cooked very simple meals on the stone fireplace on the floor. I had placed heavy gauge wire across the top of the stones where I could lay my cooking pots. I had a small two-burner gas stove that I used only to heat water for coffee or quick heating items.

This house wobbled every time there were earth tremors, which was often. It was always a frightening feeling. I'd had the house built high up so I could close in the bottom with bamboo and use the ground floor for my literacy classes. But there were so many people who wanted to come that we quickly built a bamboo-sided garage with a grass roof. It had a dual purpose. It housed my four-wheel drive Toyota that the Lord had provided for me after another missionary had purchased my Jeep; we stacked portable desk-like benches beside it. Each morning I would back the vehicle out, set up the benches, and await the arrival of my first literacy class of the day.

The students ranged in age from 9 years to gray-haired men and women—seventy-six of them altogether. It was a challenge but manageable because two Christian young men from my previous village had come along to help me. The morning class was the largest and main class. In the afternoon we'd teach a class as needed for some of the adults who had garden-work schedules. It was also needful to hold night classes for the adults who could only come then.

My Coleman lantern was our mode of light—not the best, but brighter than the light from the ground floor fire that students were accustomed to. After a while the classes grew smaller when some of the older people stopped because of bad eyesight and the need to work in their gardens, the source of all their food. At least they had bragging rights for the effort they had made.

It was thrilling to see many students learn to read and write their own language. Some of them would later learn to be literacy teachers themselves.

While in that village I shared the Good News of Jesus Christ and many of the students put their trust in Christ as their Savior. Others who weren't students also saw their need for God's free gift of salvation and placed their trust in Jesus' sacrifice for them.

Nul Kauba (Nool-cow-bah) is one who holds a special place in my memory. He was a powerful sorcerer in that area, who was feared and respected by the people. As I worked with the new believers to help them understand the wonder of their salvation and the greatness of God's attributes, we also learned to pray together for others. Nul Kauba was often the focus of our prayers, and we shared our faith with him regularly. Over time, God brought about great changes in this old, angry man.

Here's what I recorded in a prayer letter some time later:

> Nul Kauba, a former sorcerer, has proven to be a real believer in Christ and a faithful witness for Him.
> I recall the day several months ago when

Nul Kauba, holding his walking stick, came hobbling into our Sunday church service. And I well remember how the Christians got so excited that "the man like Satan" (as they called him) had come to hear God's Word. Some of us had been praying for this man, and they reminded me of that.

After the service was over, he told us that prior to that particular day he hadn't had any thoughts of God nor had he wanted to hear this "religious talk" that some mission groups were trying to persuade him to come and hear. But on this certain day he decided to come and hear "God's talk." One of the Christians began to share God's Word with him, but he confessed that Satan had blinded his mind for so long that he could not understand. He said, "My heart is like a stone, and my mind is in great darkness because I've served Satan all these years."

We realized that this was true, but we also knew that God could reveal Himself to any soul that was eager to learn of Him. So we began to teach Nul Kauba, starting with the attributes of God, and then about Satan and sin. As he began to understand, we presented the Gospel of Christ to him. God wondrously enlightened his blinded mind so he was able to see his need for a Savior and to understand God's provision for his salvation in the person of Jesus Christ. Our hearts were thrilled when a few weeks later Nul Kauba accepted Jesus Christ as his personal Savior.

I must confess that my faith was small, and I really wondered how much Nul Kauba understood of what we had taught him. I hoped that God had really reached his heart and had saved him. But today I have no doubts about his salvation. He can't read, yet he retained what we have taught him. He is also sharing it with others.

Last week it brought joy to our hearts as we heard our new brother in the Lord witnessing to another old sorcerer, clearly explaining the New Testament stories from the virgin birth to the resurrection of Christ. Evidently this man has seen a real change in Nul Kauba's life and wants to find out what has happened to him. As Nul Kauba shared his testimony, the sorcerer said that he'd like to believe in Jesus, too, and be changed like his friend. Some of the Christians who stood by listening felt rebuked for not witnessing; seeing Nul Kauba sharing his faith in Christ challenged them to do likewise.

This Sunday, the sorcerer, whose name is Mol, came again to hear God's Word, and after the service Nul Kauba took him aside and once more shared the Gospel with him.

Nul Kauba did have a hard heart, as he admitted, but I've seen him with a changed heart. Christ made the difference! This morning his wife was talking angrily to him, and although I didn't hear everything that she said, I knew it wasn't very nice. He told her that he is now a believer in Jesus Christ and didn't want to hear her "pig talk." Then he walked away from her presence. That was just another confirmation to me that this dear old man is a new creature in Christ.

Nul Kauba lives in one of the three nearby houses. He faithfully watches over me when I'm alone and watches out for my house and possessions when I'm away.

It's so rewarding to see God bring His light into the darkness, and give hope that endures.

Another outstanding memory is of the teamwork and rigorous commitment involved in the completion of the New

Testament in the Sinasina language. Chuck and Wanda Turner labored faithfully to translate the Scriptures, which amounted to more than 1,000 pages of manuscript from Matthew to Revelation. Chuck benefitted from the help of Sinasina translation helpers, and Wanda, although often in ill health, persevered in love to support her husband and see the job accomplished.

Julaine was asked to help type the manuscript which she did until she went back to Wisconsin to prepare for her wedding. Graeme Northe and I were asked to proofread the manuscript. Graeme's wife, Helen, encouraged us all. So too did Art and Stella Beatham, who cared for the practical details of maintenance, purchased and shipped supplies to missionaries, and showed hospitality.

There were no shortcuts in the translation or proofreading process. Every word was typed on a sturdy typewriter. What a job to proofread each word of the more than 1000-page manuscript! It was especially hard when decisions were made to change the spelling of some of the verbs because it meant that we needed to start over again and again. The Lord helped us day by day as we read from early morning until day's end, and even some evenings. It was both grueling and rewarding. The Turners rejoiced to be able to deliver the final manuscript to a printer in Hong Kong in 1975.

How exciting it was when those precious New Testaments arrived! Government officials, missionaries from nearby locations, as well as some of our co-workers from our international school and mission headquarters all came to help us celebrate. The Sinasina people dressed in their best tribal attire, sang songs of praise to the Lord, and gave speeches. They were so excited to finally have a personal copy of God's word in their own language. Tears of joy and gratitude were evident on many faces.

Later, the Turners would return and translate the Old Testament books of Genesis and Exodus into the Sinasina language, and once again Graeme and I would be very much involved in proofreading each word. The Sinasina leaders and

Bible teachers would be thrilled to have these Scriptures to aid them in teaching God's Word.

Every personal sacrifice that was made to share this Truth was worth it. What a privilege to see God change lives for His glory!

Prior to heading to America for my second furlough, I went to Adelaide, Australia, in order to have surgery on my nose. Thankfully my dear friends Lyall and Sue Mumford, former missionaries in PNG, invited me to stay with them. Sue was a nurse, which was an added blessing.

You will recall the toboggan accident that I had as a child, which made it difficult for me to breathe through my nose. X-rays now revealed that there were multiple fractures, which required extensive nose surgery. Have you ever seen a nose cast? Well, I was to wear one for six weeks or, I should say, until the cast fell off because the swelling had significantly decreased. On my last visit to the surgeon, he was quite amused when I pulled the cast out of my handbag. What a relief to be able to breathe through my nose again! It didn't matter that I was left with a slightly crooked nose.

When the doctor gave me the okay to travel to America, my first stop was with my brother Herbert and his wife, Mary, just north of San Diego.

As we were getting acquainted, Mary asked me, "Rosalie, how do you live?" I replied, "I live by faith." To help her understand what this meant I said, "Here is an example of living by faith. I'm here in San Diego with an airline ticket to get me to Milwaukee, Wisconsin. I have no money to go further so I either need an airline ticket or a vehicle to drive. I do not have money to buy a vehicle. I'm asking God to provide what He knows is the best for me." I further explained that, to me, it seemed that a vehicle would be best as it would allow me to visit friends in several states and accept opportunities to tell others about my ministry and the work that God was doing through New Tribes Mission in PNG.

A short while later their telephone rang. My friend and co-worker, Carol Gutwein, who was in Wisconsin wanted to talk with me. She told me that the McClarens, a former missionary couple in PNG, had offered her the use of one of their cars for her furlough needs. When she told them that her parents had already purchased a car for her to use, they asked if she knew of any missionary who needed a car. She mentioned my need. So Mr. and Mrs. McClaren were offering me the use of their spare car.

I went back and sat on the sofa beside Mary to relate this exciting news. "God is providing a car for me to use, Mary." She was speechless. I just had to say "Thank you Lord" out loud. "Mary, this can only be explained by God's faithfulness to meet my needs." The Lord works in ways that are beyond our imagination. I also shared my testimony with Mary and my brother before I left. I continued to ask God to open their understanding to see their need for a personal relationship with the Savior.

As soon as possible, I made arrangements to fly from Milwaukee to Indianapolis where the McClarens met me. I stayed the night with them, and then drove off toward Connecticut in their beautiful Oldsmobile, making stops along the way. When I reached my destination, another wonderful surprise awaited me.

A dear lady made her lovely home available to me—it was about five miles from my church and near to my brother Carlton's family. At that time she was caring for an elderly lady in another home. She not only gave me the house keys, but had put a large sum of money in an envelope under my pillow for me to stock the cupboards and refrigerator with food. What a blessing and provision from the Lord! Later I was able to return the blessing and drive her to New Brunswick, Canada, to visit her sister.

Chapter 19

The Last Years with My Sinasina People

After a short furlough, I returned to work with the Sinasina people in October 1976. I was excited at the challenges ahead, which would include giving help with translation projects and doing a thorough revision of our Sinasina primers. It would be necessary to teach a trial class to test the new primer books, so I'll begin there.

First I needed to choose a sizeable group of young people ages 6 to 15 years old, who wanted to learn to read and write their own language. Before starting the twelve-week class I warned them that they would have to work very hard with little time to play, because I would soon be going to another village to use the primers.

During the selection process, I met a small child named Dom, possibly 6 or 7 years old, who eagerly wanted to attend the school. His size made it appear that he was too young so I told him that he would have to wait until he was older. Tears came to his eyes as he pleaded with me to let him come. So I used the same exercise that teachers did in the government schools to determine if he was old enough. "Put your hand over the top of your head and touch your other ear," I instructed him. So he tried several times with each hand, but he could barely touch his other ear. That meant that he was too young.

But Dom wouldn't take no for an answer. Once again tears welled up in his eyes, and he pleaded with me to let him attend. So I gave in and said, "Okay, I will let you try out on the first day or two." To make a long story short, Dom excelled in school, as did several of his brothers and sisters who also attended that first class. Their father was the church pastor and he was very proud, especially on the day when they received their reading and writing certificates. The revised primers were indeed successful.

Along with literacy instruction, I shared the Good News of Jesus Christ as always with each of the students. One by one these kids accepted Jesus Christ as their personal Savior. After that I taught them the Bible basics. They memorized a lot of verses, and by the end of the twelve-week class they were able to read from the New Testament. It was amazing to behold! We held a special graduation program so the parents and others in their village could attend. Each student took part in saying memorized Bible verses and singing. I had to have Dom stand on a little table so everyone could see him. He stood there with a microphone, hooked up to my computer, around his neck as he read from the book of Romans. I was so proud of Dom, as were his parents. His mom and others cried as they heard this little guy read so well. He definitely was above average and I can see why he wanted to come to school so badly. It made me think back to my early school years.

As the literacy class ended, the government school in the area had started a new year. Dom wanted to go to that school so his parents asked if I would talk with the school teacher, which I did. When he saw Dom, the verdict was no; he was too small, which meant too young; besides that, the class had already started. I explained that the boy was above average, and I more or less assured the teacher that this kid would do well even if he was late in starting. So I paid the school fee and Dom began his first year in a government school.

It turned out that Dom had an advantage over the other students in school; he had learned the phonetics of his native language so this helped him when the class studied the trade language of Melanesian Pidgin. This little boy excelled so quickly that he was advanced to the second year. Long after I had left the tribe, his parents came up with the money for him to continue and, with the help of missionaries, Dom graduated from high school. I was told that he was an exceptional student and did well even in the English language. He also went to a Bible school in a town some distance away from the tribe and did very well. He took joy in living for the Lord and sharing the Gospel. Sometime after that he became very ill with cancer and died. I understand that his life testimony truly glorified God.

Dom's parents were broken-hearted. At one point they were so sad that they wanted to go into a cave and die because he was their very special and youngest son. However, they turned in their sadness to God for His comfort, and took courage because they knew that Dom was in Heaven with the Savior he loved and served.

After completing this trial class, I moved to different villages to further test the new primers. My next destination was halfway between the Sinasina tribe and another tribe. I was driven along the Highlands Highway and dropped off at a place where I could begin my hike down the mountain into the valley.

Missionary Art Beatham helped build a nice bush house for me in Kai village—it even had a corrugated tin roof. Drinking water was scarce in that area, so the tin roof ensured that rain could run off the roof into a good-sized container. A large schoolroom was constructed that also served as the church meeting place. This time my literacy classes were made up of a few younger students and many adults who wanted to learn to read so they could then read God's Word in their own language. I had a wonderful ministry in that village for many months.

Even though these people spoke yet another dialect of the main Sinasina language, most of them did very well in the literacy classes. As in the other villages, some of the older people found the studies too difficult but they enjoyed trying. Many people also trusted Jesus Christ as their Savior. Sadly, some later fell by the wayside. This is often the situation in tribal work, especially when the outside world encroaches and tempts the people with drinking, gambling, and other vices. Some who turned away would later respond to the Lord's chastisement and become a delight to work with, while others caused us to wonder about their relationship to Jesus Christ. One day we will know who were truly born again.

From mid-1967 through late1979 I lived in eight villages in the Sinasina tribe. In each location I set up literacy schools and taught young people and adults who wanted to learn to read and write in their own language. The Lord also gave me opportunities to share His message and then disciple any believers in the basics concerning their walk with the Lord and how to depend on His promises. To His glory, many came to know Jesus Christ as their personal Savior.

Recently, I reread a prayer letter from that time. It was difficult for me to say my last goodbye to this special group of people. I felt sad, too, for the people in Gunange because they still needed a missionary man to be willing to go to that remote village to disciple the men who were promising leaders, and to encourage the acting leaders. Thankfully, my prayer was answered when Graeme and Helen Northe, with their family, moved to that village to do exactly that until they later returned to New Zealand.

For a few months preceding my furlough, I moved into a different tribal group to live with my friend and co-worker-to-be, Carol Gutwein, while she was checking the New Testament that she had translated for the Yagaria people. It was a completely different language from the Sinasina language, but I could communicate with most of the younger people by using the Melanesian Pidgin trade language. The Turners had been working on a Sinasina concordance so I helped them with that project. At that time neither Carol nor I were in good health, but we persevered to complete what we felt we needed to do before going to America on furlough.

During the first months of that medical furlough both of us were very sick. I was able to stay at the New Tribes Bible

Institute in Waukesha, Wisconsin, where Carol's parents served on staff. Several times each week I traveled back and forth to Milwaukee for special treatments; at the same time I stayed on a limited healthy diet—not what I wanted to do, but I was desperate. In fact, when the people who were attending to me realized that I planned to return to PNG, they told Carol that I would not come back to the USA alive. Well, I did get better and I lived in that country for several more years.

Carol's health was also renewed. She and I would soon begin a new phase of life in PNG, but before I continue with that part of my story, let's take time to experience God's care in some hair-raising situations.

Chapter 20

Bountiful Protection

God has taken care of me in some very unique ways and in some difficult situations. Often He used my dear tribal brothers and sisters to help me when I was too sick to help myself. From the start, they chose to call me Ningege (neen-gay-gay) which is the name of a food that I loved to eat, but there is nothing similar to it in America. In the Sinasina tribe they use names of almost anything below or above the ground, or in the sky to name their children.

When I lived over the mountain in Gunange, the roads were often so bad that I had to make my own bridges and dig out of landslides before I could reach the village. One time I was very weak and almost delirious with a very high fever from malaria. In the early evening I summoned the people to come to my house, especially my village papa and mama, because I needed to give them some instructions. As I lay on the bed burning up with fever and shaking with chills, I explained that my papa and mama should check on me in the morning to see if I was okay. "Speak to me first through the bamboo walls," I told them. "If I don't answer, break down the door and check on me."

As it turned out, the people checked on me that evening and several times early the next morning. My tribal papa kept watch outside. He'd come to the side of the wall where I was laying and scratch on the bamboo. I could hear him sobbing as he asked, "Ningege, are you there?" meaning, "Ningege, are you still alive?" I answered that I was, but still very sick and weak.

The men decided to make a stretcher from bush materials to carry me over the mountain to our main mission station. They hoped to catch a ride with a truck that might be traveling on the better side of the mountain road. But by morning I was feeling somewhat better after the malaria medicine had started to do its work. As weak as I was, and with several people traveling with me, I drove my vehicle up over the mountain and down the other side to our mission station where I could recover. I have precious memories of the love and kindness shown to me at that time, and in so many other ways by these dear people.

I later experienced another severe bout of malaria in Kai village, across the valley near another tribe. This time there were no roads to drive on from the village. High fever and chills made it unlikely that I could hike from my house in the valley up the mountain to get to a road, hoping to be picked up by a missionary from the mission station.

Once again my dear village brothers came to my rescue and piggy-backed me up a steep mountain as I clung to their necks. Others followed, crying along the way. Several of them have since gone to Heaven, and I look forward to seeing them again someday. I'm sure I'll want to hug and thank them again for all of their kindness shown to me. They were such loving and giving people who would have done anything for me, and I felt the same toward them.

You will recall the time when I went to the coastal town of Lae accompanied by my Christian brother, Josia, and when my Jeep broke down and went up in smoke after we arrived at our destination. Well, several years later, we had another bad experience on that same road; however, it did have a funny ending.

Josia and I were heading back from Lae, where we'd purchased supplies and I had my vehicle repaired. We were traveling on that long stretch of bumpy and dusty highway with only a short distance to go before we would begin the climb up the mountain. Trouble reared its head as we approached a bridge that we would have to cross. Five men were lined up across the bridge entrance. My heart started to thump because I knew they were up to no good. On the radio news we often heard of such holdups along the main highways, especially on the Highlands Highway. Josia, my personal guard, was filled with fear. I was too!

The Lord has created me with the ability to think and respond quickly in difficult situations, for which I am thankful. I'd also prepared myself for possible danger on the highway and other places by purchasing a megaphone to carry around with me. And guess what? I thought quickly enough to grab it and blow my train whistle imitation—and it was loud! Those men took a dive off the bridge and began running down under it as Josia and I sped over the top. We were shaken and I was fighting hard to drive with my emotions at a high level, but as we started to climb the mountain, we kept thanking our wonderful God for His protection. He had saved us once again from what could have been a very bad situation.

Remember I explained before that God had gifted me with the ability to imitate sounds. The train whistle has not only been used to protect me but also to entertain others. No one can understand how I can make that noise. I have blown my whistle for dignitaries, at conventions, in unusual places, and for the most unlikely people. More often than not, I end up with an opportunity to share the Good News of Jesus Christ.

After that scary encounter on the Highlands Highway, I purchased a flashlight which had a switch that allowed me to turn on a sound like a police siren. On another occasion I used it in what appeared to be another potential holdup. When I turned on that siren and blasted it through my megaphone, the approaching criminals fled to the bushes while I sped on my way shouting thanks to our God!

Another possible life-and-death highway situation took place sometime later. Mol, a church pastor, and his wife, Monika, had prayed for a son for many years after having four girls. So when Eremuge (Air-ray-moo-gay) was born, he was very special. When he was small, he became sick with a high fever, which lasted several days. On Sunday he seemed to be getting worse so after the church service his parents asked me if I would take him to the hospital. Off we went in my vehicle on an emergency trip to the little hospital in the small town of Kundiawa.

Thankfully, the clinic was open for emergencies on Sundays. The staff gave Eremuge medicine and sent extra along to treat him in the days ahead, so we were able to head back to the village that same day. We were about halfway home along the Highlands Highway and beginning to climb a somewhat winding area of the road when my eyes saw something that frightened me.

Just ahead on a high hillside stood three fierce looking men with their faces painted black. They kept staring at our vehicle, then with their homemade shotguns pointed at us, they started to run down the high embankment toward us. I knew that they used large spike nails for bullets in those homemade guns. Their intent was to stop us in order to rob us, or even worse. Once again I was able to think quickly. "Get down," I shouted to Mol, who was holding his sick little boy. I ducked my head and kept driving, hoping that we wouldn't go into the side of the mountain or off the highway. Again the Lord protected us. The men did not stop us. Their aim evidently missed us and we arrived home safely.

Next day we heard that the men had tried to hold up a small passenger bus that came behind us but, as they were boarding it, a police vehicle came along and the three men jumped off. Two of them got away, but the police shot the other in the leg and he ended up in the hospital. Generally, police did not patrol that highway on Sundays. How grateful we were for God's intervention once again.

Sometime in the 1980's a hair-raising ordeal occurred on what was supposed to be a short, relaxing break at a northern coastal area of the country. Carol and I had just completed a busy schedule of travel to various tribal areas where we helped our co-workers with Bible translation and literacy. We planned to enjoy the sandy beach where snorkeling on an inner tube was great fun, before returning to the Highlands region.

On this particular day we parked the mission vehicle and walked toward the beach. No one was there except for a man who was standing on a tree limb that hung out over the water; he was looking for fish to spear. We noticed that he left when Carol and I started down the beach to look for pretty sea-shells. However, she went one way and I went the opposite.

After awhile I turned around to go back to the car when I thought I heard someone calling my name in the distance. I started to walk faster and soon realized that indeed it was my name, and it was Carol's voice. As I got closer I saw Carol on her knees in the sand with a native man standing straddled over her with a large spear lifted over her head as if he was going to spear her. I took off running at an amazing pace, with my quick thinking mind telling me to swing around behind him and grab him by the neck.

Before I could do that, the man stood up, turned toward me with a fierce look, lifted his long spear, and pointed it straight at me. Don't ask me why, but I stopped and rapidly waved my hand back and forth in front of him. In a moment he turned his spear away from me and pointed it toward the ground. All I can say is that God filled me with holy courage. I walked over to Carol as he stepped aside, picked up her glasses from the sand, and grabbed her hand to help her up.

"Let's go," I said to her. I kept holding her hand as we started to walk away at a rapid pace toward the car. "Don't look back! Don't look back!" I kept repeating. We had no idea if the madman was following us or not. When I nervously tried to open the car door it wouldn't open; my heart felt like it went up to my throat! I thought about putting my fist through the window but the vision of a broken hand deterred me. Instead, I twisted and shook the door handle some more and the door opened. Carol and I wheeled out of there in a hurry, not knowing where the spear-man was. I was so emotionally shaken that I could hardly drive. That night we were both emotionally drained, but our hearts and lips were filled with praise to our wonderful God. He'd intervened and saved us from a near tragic ending.

The Lord has shown His greatness, compassion, and perfect timing in protecting me and others. My heart rejoices in Him. He has also opened doors to share the Gospel of His dear Son in many places. His love is so great that He sent Jesus to give His life and to shed His precious blood to pay the price for the sins of all the people of the world. To me it's worth giving my soul, my life, and my all to take that message of salvation to people without hope, whether at home or around the world.

Were the whole realm of nature mine,
that were an offering far too small;
love so amazing, so divine,
demands my soul, my life, my all.
—Isaac Watts

Chapter 21

A New Location

$\mathcal{A}$t the end of our medical furlough in 1980, it was wonderful to return to PNG and get settled into a new house with Carol at the mission headquarters. She and I were grateful for those who worked hard to build that house for us while we were in the USA. It was made of recycled timber, and it had electricity and an inside toilet—something I had never had in all the years that I worked in the Sinasina tribe. Another blessing was better roads which meant less wear and tear on my vehicle.

Having Carol as my co-worker was a very special answer to my prayers. For part of my previous term, I had worked alone because Julaine got married. For about two and a half years I kept asking God if I could be a co-worker with Carol Gutwein, because I recognized that she was an extremely committed worker. Realistically speaking, there was no reason why it would work out. I say this because Carol excelled academically and was involved in a ministry that I was not trained or gifted in. The interesting thing is that toward the end of my time among the Sinasina people, Carol came for two weeks to check the translation of the Old Testament book of Exodus with the translator—and she stayed at my house.

During one of our conversations, she asked me where I was planning to work when I returned to that country, since missionaries would no longer be needed among the Sinasina tribe. A literacy program was in place with trained teachers, and several ordained pastors were ministering faithfully. I had lived and worked with the people for twelve and a half years and was no longer needed.

In answer to Carol's question I said that I'd probably go to our mission headquarters where I hoped to teach literacy to the village people in the surrounding area. Carol had finished translating the New Testament into the language of the Yagaria people, so she was also planning to move to the mission headquarters.

Then she asked, "Would you live there with me?" I thought "Hello!" and replied, "I've been praying about this for nearly two and half years." She said, "You have not." I enthusiastically replied, "Yes I have!" And to prove it I told her to go to my desk and get my Bible. I opened it to Psalm 37:4-5: "Delight thyself also in the Lord; and he shall give thee the desires of thine heart. Commit thy way unto the Lord; trust also in him; and he shall bring it to pass." I pointed to her initials that I'd written beside those verses, and the date that I started praying. I believed that God would fulfill my heart's desire to have Carol as my co-worker—in His time, of course, just like He had opened a door for me to enter missionary training to serve Him full-time back in 1964.

When our NTM leaders agreed to this arrangement, it was the beginning of Carol and me sharing a house together for twelve years in PNG. God had miraculously answered another prayer! We often traveled together to assist missionary teams in different tribal areas—Carol as a Bible translation consultant and I as a literacy consultant.

Being a literacy consultant wasn't anything that I ever thought I could do. When the leaders first asked me to consider that job, I responded, "Me? Be a literacy consultant? I don't know how to do that." They commented on the success of the literacy program among the Sinasina people at that time, and wanted me to help missionaries working in other languages whenever they were ready to start their literacy programs. I thought for a moment and said, "I don't know how to be a literacy consultant, but I can tell them what I did." "That's what we want you to do," came the reply. I was okay with that. The leaders seemed to have confidence in me so I decided that I would put my heart and soul into this challenging new ministry.

Often I'm asked if I speak all thirty-eight of the languages in PNG where I went to work with the teams. Of course the answer is "No." Before I arrived in each tribe, the team was required to have a dictionary of their tribal language and the English equivalent. From that they provided word lists that I'd look through in search of possible combinations of usable words with which we could create complete sentences. Starting with the most elementary words, we built very simple sentences and progressively added new words as we moved from one primer to the next. The method I prefer to use is progressive and predictive, but for some languages with complicated grammar we often needed to make an exception to that. Without a dictionary, or at least detailed word lists, I would not have been able to help them.

It was fun for me to hand print "syllable" as well as "word" flash cards for most of the languages where I worked. The cards were an important part of each teaching lesson. The daily lessons involved blackboard syllable drills. Syllables were then reinforced with flash card drills. The drills were followed by the students reading the same sounds and words in their primer books. Writing followed, which helped to strengthen what they had just read.

The method worked well in most languages. A successful literacy program depended on several things: a settled orthography (alphabet) with good primers, motivated students, and good teachers. Each missionary team should be involved in this, or at least in agreement with the program, even though their personal ministry might be concentrated on another aspect of the work, such as translating Scripture or teaching Bible lessons.

Prior to being asked to do the consultant work, I'd been teaching young people and adults who lived near the headquarters to read. I was also teaching a religious instruction class at a government community school nearby. Those kids came to our house after school to learn more about the Bible. Most of them accepted Jesus Christ as their personal Savior and continued to come after school for further teaching.

My heart was sad when I saw the need to give up that ministry. The consultant work required a lot of preparation for my travels to tribal locations scattered across the country to help our missionaries with their literacy programs. Each time I got home, I would work on writing the teacher's manual for that particular language. Once that was completed, I began to prepare for the next trip. It was always a joy and privilege to serve my fellow missionaries and the people with whom they worked.

Carol and I also traveled to other countries in Africa, Asia, and South America to help people in our areas of expertise. Booking flights to such places from PNG meant that tickets were costly and travel itineraries were not dependable. But God always took care of us, and we always found the work rewarding that He had equipped us to do.

Some years later, we were asked to relocate once again. This time it would be to our organization's home offices in Sanford, Florida. We left the country in 1992 but would return periodically to teach seminars and train more consultants. We never lacked for work when we returned to PNG.

Chapter 22

Here and There

When I arrived in Los Angeles in 1992, I had no vehicle so was met by my brother Herbert who lived near San Diego. From there I went to the home of my dear friends, Gary and Donna Coombs, who lived El Cajon. Donna navigated me around the city and arranged for me to see a specialist. Towards the end of my time in PNG, I had intense pain in my eye, jaw, and ear. After x-rays and other tests, it was determined that I had a severe TMJ problem, partly because I had osteo-arthritis in my jaw. The specialist recommended that I visit a prosthodontist in Missouri, where I was heading.

After visiting with friends in the area, I was driven to the home of a very special elderly couple, Earl and Olive Grove, in Venice, California, who had always wanted me to visit them. We had a unique connection because one of their sons, Dave, had been a missionary in the Sinasina tribe before I had arrived there. Steve, their other son, was visiting his parents when I arrived. He had evidently been talking to a new Christian about me. This guy had been saved out of a rough life and had since grown in the Lord. Steve felt like I should talk with this gentleman, Mike, who now lived in Spokane, Washington with his wife and children. So he rang Mike and after talking to him for a short time, he handed the phone to me.

After the brief formalities, Mike said out of the blue, "Do you want a car?" I certainly did, so I answered, "Yes, I'd love to have a car, but where would I get one?" At this point I had no prospects of buying one, so I certainly wasn't expecting to hear Mike's answer. "I have a car that I'll give you if you can come here to pick it up." I thought, "Wow! Thank you Lord for yet another blessing!"

Mike told me that if I'd fly into Spokane he'd meet me at the airport and take me to the motor vehicle department where I could pay the $5.00 tax for the transfer of the registration into my name. All I could say was thank you to him and praise the Lord! I don't remember what year the Buick La Sabre was, but I do know that it was a tremendous blessing. It meant I could stop to visit with friends on my journey to Columbia, Missouri, where I would stay for several weeks with the Gutwein family.

From there I made the two-hour trip to the University of Missouri School of Dentistry in Kansas City several times each week. Students and an experienced prosthodontist provided special teeth to take care of my TMJ problem, so my dental needs were taken care of at a minimal cost versus the high cost of normal prosthodontist care. The pain in my face and jaw diminished and then went away completely. Thank you Lord!

Meanwhile, in Sanford, Florida, a duplex was being prepared for Carol and me at the NTM Homes, a retirement center. She would live in one side and I in the other. We hoped it would become a refuge for us after the long, hard overseas journeys that would become part of our ministry as international consultants in Bible translation and literacy to missionary teams worldwide. We were starting from scratch as far as household items went, but the Lord provided for us through His people so we were able to buy some necessary items and move in.

We had been there only a couple of days when Carol and I were invited to meet her sister and husband at a Chinese restaurant a few miles down the road. After a nice meal and visit, they needed to get back to the hotel where they were staying, and I was eager to get home in order to hear an election debate that night.

Because I was having trouble at night with my eyes, Carol

drove my Buick back from the restaurant. As soon as we parked in the driveway, I hurried inside and left Carol to lock it up. While I was trying to adjust the picture on the television, I heard a loud scream. At first I thought that it was coming from across the street, where people may have been drinking and fighting. But it didn't take me long to figure out that the scream was coming from the other direction. Then I heard a car horn blowing too—and it was my car horn!

Out the door I went as fast as I could go. Sure enough, a man had come across the property to the carport just as Carol was opening the door. He had grabbed her bag and given her his fist right between the eyes. She was somewhat traumatized, and my adrenaline was pumping hard as I tried to help her out of the car and into the house. What an introduction to our new apartments!

We called the police and informed our leaders, who quickly arrived. Of course, the thief had run off in a hurry with Carol's handbag. But typical of Carol, who was a very organized person, she called her parents in Missouri to report the loss of her credit cards and her driver's license. During the next two nights men from the mission stood watch to make sure that nothing else happened to us, and probably to calm our rattled nerves. Carol's neck was strained from the hard blow to her face. Next day her face was swollen, and it was black and blue around her eyes, nose, and cheeks. We all felt so sorry for her, but she was a real trooper through it all.

I felt very vulnerable. Our place was close to the road and there was no fence yet because our building was at the newest end of the complex. So I told Carol, "I'm not staying in this house any longer because I do not feel safe here." We contacted our leaders to ask if we could move temporarily to an apartment in the mission's main office complex nearby. They agreed, and even helped move our things to the one empty apartment that was available. We felt safe there until we left for our next overseas ministry trip. When we returned to the USA, we were able to relocate to a different duplex on the other side of the mission's retirement center; it became a refuge indeed.

From the early 1990s we traveled to different ethnic groups on three continents, continuing the same ministries in which we'd been involved in PNG—helping missionaries with Bible translation and literacy. Carol and I traveled together at first, but later, when she had completed her work in some of the areas, I often traveled alone. I had the opportunity to work in an additional thirty plus language groups.

Meeting new missionary teams, and working with them with the hope of helping them create good literacy programs thrilled me. Some methods worked better in some languages, but not so well in another, and that could be for various reasons just like it was in PNG. Likewise, teams in other countries sometimes had to revise their primers because of a change in the orthography. It's been a wonderful privilege and experience to serve my fellow missionaries and to meet many tribal people worldwide.

In the late 1990s the Sinasina church leaders contacted me to ask if I would come back to the tribe and work with them to translate lessons from the Building on Firm Foundations series into their language. Those lessons were not available to them in the earlier years when we were there in the tribe.

This chronological set of 70 lessons starts "in the beginning" and reveals the Creator through His stories that are recorded in His Word—the Bible. As people listen to Old Testament stories, they soon learn about who God is, the creation, man's fall into sin, God's law, His punishment for sin, and His promise of a deliverer. When they hear the New Testament stories of Jesus birth, ministry, death, burial, and resurrection, many believe God's Word and understand that Jesus is the deliverer. He is their Savior!

The Sinasina leaders had heard how well the missionaries were doing in the more recent language groups where they were teaching these lessons—many people were trusting Jesus for their salvation. My first response was that I was too busy traveling around the world with my ministry. Besides that, it had been around twenty years since I had used their language regularly. They assured me that I would be able to help them. God gave me His peace and I accepted the challenge. So I began thinking about the practical side of living with my Sinasina brothers and sisters once again.

I would need a place to live and equipment to use, such as a computer, printer, power source, generator, batteries, and basic household items. So I made a list and decided to include some of the needs in a prayer letter. It was amazing how dear Christian friends and some churches rallied behind me. They sent the funds for me to purchase everything I needed to build a nice bush house and furnish it with all the necessary equipment. It was overwhelming, and my heart was filled with thanksgiving to God. The Lord even supplied solar panels for night lighting and a generator, plus extra items to make it easier for us.

I continued to travel to other countries helping missionary teams with their literacy programs, and in between those trips I tried to squeeze in several months each year to work with the Sinasina leaders, translating the series of the Firm Foundation teaching lessons. They were the main translators and quite capable, but they needed someone to scrutinize their spelling especially, as well as check for any omissions and for clarity of the text of each lesson. Finally, we proofread every lesson several times before it went to be printed. We eventually translated even more Bible lessons that covered all the books of the New Testament.

During that time I was called a "workhorse," but the people wanted these lessons so badly that they were willing to work long hours when it was necessary. We would never have finished otherwise. It was a great encouragement to know that many people were praying for us.

One of my life's challenging verses continues to be: "Therefore, my beloved brethren, be ye stedfast, unmoveable, always abounding in the work of the Lord, forasmuch as ye know that your labor is not in vain in the Lord" (1 Corinthians 15:58).

* * * * * * * * * * * *

My mind goes back to my first furlough and a visit that I had with an elderly lady whom I believe was a born again Christian; she was also one of my mother's best friends. I told her about the ministry I was doing and showed her some pictures of the people and places where I worked. Then we chatted for quite a while.

At one point I noticed tears in her eyes, which puzzled me. "Did I say something to make you feel bad?" I asked. She answered, "No, Rosalie, but I must tell you this. Just before your mother passed away, I was visiting with her and she was holding you in her arms. She looked at me with hope in her eyes and said, 'Coris, I don't know why, but I feel like this little girl is going to be someone special.'"

Why she said that I may never know, but I do know that being an ambassador for my Lord and Savior to the uttermost parts of the earth is pretty special.

Clarifying Facts

*M*y foster home mother sometimes went to church, but I do not know if she ever trusted Christ as her personal Savior, although it seems that she had a religious leaning. I hope she did, and if so I'll see her in Heaven where we will be one in Christ, and I may want to thank her for her patience with me. Otherwise, the rest of my experiences in her home are in the sea of God's forgetfulness, and like the song says, "That's good enough for me."

* * * * * * * * * * * * *

Sometime in my early twenties I began to visit my father again whenever I returned to Swan's Island. By then he had quit drinking for health reasons. My most vivid memory is of the day we said good-bye for the last time, just before I went to New Guinea for my first term. We hugged each other and then he said, "I'm sorry, dear, that I failed you as a father." I knew that was not easy for him to tell me. My reply went something like this: "Dad, that's okay. God has forgiven me and changed my life. He's filled my heart with love instead of hatred. I love you and hope you too will come to know His forgiveness before it's too late."

Before I opened the door to leave, he asked when my "Unshackled" story was going to be on the radio, and on what station. I knew it would be on a Christian radio station but I didn't know the exact date as that varied from state to state. I explained that in order to tell the story of my life I had to share the difficult things about our relationship in our earlier years... and I would rather he didn't hear it because it would hurt him.

My sister later told me that Dad did listen to the program and had remarked, "I'm proud of her for telling the truth." He knew a lot about the Bible, but he seemed to keep his distance by calling most Christians hypocrites. I never saw my father again but I wrote to him from New Guinea. In the last letter that I sent to him when he was dying of cancer, I exhorted him at some length to stop hiding behind the hypocrites because God would take care of them. Instead, I pleaded with him to accept God's Son as his personal Savior before it would be eternally too late. His soul could only go to one of two places— Heaven or Hell—and I wanted to see him in Heaven. My sister said he carried that letter around in his back pocket.

When he was in the hospital, near death's door, I understand that a family member requested the pastor of a small Baptist church in coastal Maine to visit my father, which he did. Evidently, Dad didn't want that pastor to share anything with him from the Bible. Instead, he would always change the subject to his missionary daughter who was in New Guinea.

Well, that pastor made it known that he wanted me to contact him when I returned to the USA for my first furlough in 1971, which I did just a few months later. That's when he told me about the complete change that was evident in my father during the last few weeks of his life. My brother also noticed a significant change in our dad. I hope I'll see him in Heaven someday, along with the mother I never knew. I've been told that she was a Christian.

* * * * * * * * * * * *

It is important for me to state that I have nothing but praise for my home sending church family of the First Baptist Church in Waterford, Connecticut, who became deeply involved in my life and ministry. Nor can I praise the Lord enough for all that they have meant to me, as they have stood behind me with their prayers and support these many years. Actually, they were so eager to see me come back for my first furlough that I, in my kidding way, told some people that I was afraid they would have a statue of "Saint Rosalie" standing in the corner. That joking comment showed the contrast between their earlier hesitation at the idea of me going into missionary work and their amazing affirmation once they could see that it was God who had opened the door for me to serve Him in PNG.

Others from my church have followed me into missionary work and have served in needy places worldwide. One little spark can light a fire that spreads so far. Praise God that He has led others to see the need to follow the Lord in reaching lost souls for Christ at home and around the world.

Across the years, the Lord has given me a large family of fathers, mothers, brothers, and sisters who have made up for all that I lost out on during my childhood and teenage years. All I can say is thank you, Lord, for a wonderful loving and caring family—the family of God that I have entered into. Praise God we'll be together for all eternity. What more could I possibly ask for? Nothing! Thank you Jesus!

* * * * * * * * * * * * *

Last but not least, I am most grateful to New Tribes Mission for believing that God could use me, however He chose. Even with my limited education, God opened doors for me to be His servant in the uttermost parts of the earth. Someone has said, "God has not put a premium on education, nor has He put a premium on ignorance." I longed for an education but that was not to be, but I did become a dedicated child of His through faith in Jesus Christ, His beloved Son, who came to give His life a ransom for my soul and the souls of all mankind.

It's my prayer that you, too, will come to know Him as your personal Savior if you have not yet by faith accepted Him. Please don't put it off until it's forever too late!

If you have trusted Jesus as your personal Savior, I urge

you to live for Him. Allow Him to use your God-given gifts and abilities for His glory!

To everyone, I affirm the importance of pursuing your education, as you have the privilege to do so. Please allow God to direct you into His perfect will. He cares for you. You will find true meaning and purpose in serving Him with all your heart.

CPSIA information can be obtained at www.ICGtesting.com
Printed in the USA
LVOW040358130612

285818LV00002B/3/P